SAS® INTRODUCTORY GUIDE
Third Edition

SAS INSTITUTE INC.
BOX 8000
CARY, NORTH CAROLINA, USA 27511-8000

Jane T. Helwig edited the *SAS® Introductory Guide.*

Editorial support for the third edition was provided by **Brenda C. Kalt**. Proofing was provided by **Frances A. Kienzle**.

Composition was provided by **Susan M. Henderson** and **Stephanie H. Townsend** with production assistance provided by **Lisa N. Clements** under the direction of **Carol M. Thompson**.

The correct bibliographic citation for this manual is as follows: *SAS® Introductory Guide*. Third Edition. Cary, NC: SAS Institute Inc., 1985. 99 pp.

SAS® Introductory Guide.

86 85 4 3 2 1

Base SAS® software, the foundation of the SAS System, provides data retrieval and management, programming, statistical, and reporting capabilities. Also in the SAS System are SAS/GRAPH,® SAS/FSP,® SAS/ETS,® SAS/IMS-DL/I,® SAS/IML,™ SAS/AF,™ SAS/OR,™ and SAS/REPLAY-CICS™ software. These products and SYSTEM 2000® Data Base Management System, including the Multi-User,™ QueX,™ Screen Writer,™ CREATE,™ and CICS interface products, are available from SAS Institute Inc. a private company devoted to the support and further development of the software and related services. *SAS Communications,® SAS Training,® SAS Views,®* and the SASware Ballot® are published by SAS Institute Inc.

Preface

This book had its origins in 1972, when I noticed that computer novices could begin to use the SAS® System productively after ten minutes of explanation. Translating these ten minutes of explanation to written words resulted in the *SAS Introductory Guide*.

The scope of the *SAS Introductory Guide* was defined in large part through conversations with the late William C. Reynolds, of the University of North Carolina at Chapel Hill; and J. Philip Miller of Washington University in St. Louis.

Appreciation is also due Kathryn A. Council, who wrote Chapter 11 on analysis of variance; John P. Sall, who wrote Chapter 12 on regression; and Alice T. Allen, who wrote Appendix 1 on the SAS System at your site.

The comments and suggestions of James H. Goodnight and Anthony J. Barr were invaluable. Daniel M. Chilko's helpful explanations contributed much to the sections dealing with statistical topics.

Should errors be found in the text, we at SAS Institute would greatly appreciate being notified of them.

I hope that whether you are new to computers and data analysis, or whether you are a seasoned professional, you will be able to use and enjoy SAS software after you have read the *SAS Introductory Guide*.

Jane T. Helwig

Contents

Chapter 7

Picturing Your Data Using
PROC CHART and PROC PLOT 37

Chapter 8

Frequencies and Crosstabulations
Using PROC FREQ 45

Chapter 9

Summarizing Your Data with PROC MEANS 49

Chapter 10

Getting Correlations Using PROC CORR 53

Chapter 11
Analysis of Variance 55

Chapter 12
Regression 61

Chapter 13

Writing Custom-Tailored Reports 73

Appendix 1

Getting Started: The SAS® System at Your Installation 85

Appendix 2

More about SAS® Software 91

Chapter 1

Introduction to the SAS® System

This book's goal is to help your learn enough about the SAS System so that you can use it to get the answers you need, quickly.

What this book is about

To do simple data analyses, you need only a few of the many SAS capabilities. This book explains these capabilities so that you can begin using SAS software immediately.

You'll learn how to describe your data to the SAS System and how to request a data analysis. You will learn ways of manipulating your data. And you will learn how to produce reports in the form you want them.

But this book is only an introduction. It contains a small fraction of the information about SAS that you will find in the *SAS User's Guide: Basics* and *SAS User's Guide: Statistics*.

What this book isn't about

SAS software is useful with all kinds of data—data from experiments in the physical sciences; social science data; business data; agricultural data; marketing data—in short, any kind of data. So this book isn't oriented to any one area.

This book teaches SAS programming, not statistics. Although SAS software is an important statistical tool, explaining the concepts behind its statistical computations is beyond the scope of this book.

If you don't understand when a given statistical test should be used or how to interpret the results, a good statistics text is a necessity.

How to use this book   If you have never used computers to analyze data, you should read

- the rest of this chapter, which introduces the SAS System
- Chapter 2, which tells how to describe your data to SAS
- Chapter 4, which explains how to use SAS procedures
- Appendix 1, which describes what you need to know about your computer installation in order to use the SAS System.

Then you can read other chapters as you need them. For example, if you want to make some changes in your data values, you can read Chapter 3 on data handling. If you want descriptive statistics, you can read Chapter 9 on the MEANS procedure.

When you come to a section that doesn't apply to your data, skip it.

Important facts about SAS appear in boxes. Experienced computer users may want to skim the first four chapters, paying particular attention to the boxes.

What is the SAS System?

> The SAS System is a software system for data analysis.

Let's take that sentence apart to explain what the SAS System does.

Software system   A software system is a group of computer programs that work together. Because SAS is a system, you don't have to prepare one computer job to plot data values, another job to perform a regression, another job to print a special report. You can do it all in one SAS job.

Data   Data values are letters or numbers on disk or tape or punched cards. These letters and numbers represent information. For example, the letter F on a tape containing the results of a questionnaire survey might mean, "The respondent who gave these answers was female."

Analysis   After the data have been collected and entered onto disk or tape or cards, you are ready for data analysis—checking the data for errors, using statistical tests, and printing the results. You can use SAS for all these phases of data analysis.

Your data   Before you can describe your data to SAS, you need a clear idea of what your data represent.

For example, let's say you want to study physical measurements of the people in a certain classroom. For each of the nineteen students, you write down his or her name, sex, age, height in inches, and weight in pounds. When you finish, the information looks like figure 1-1.

Data values   Each of the items you recorded—John's sex, Janet's weight, Barbara's height—is a **data value**.

NAME	SEX	AGE	HEIGHT	WEIGHT
ALFRED	M	14	69	112
ALICE	F	13	56	84
BERNADETTE	F	13	65	98
BARBARA	F	14	62	102
HENRY	M	14	63	102
JAMES	M	12	57	83
JANE	F	12	59	84
JANET	F	15	62	112
JEFFREY	M	13	62	84
JOHN	M	12	59	99
JOYCE	F	11	51	50
JUDY	F	14	64	90
LOUISE	F	12	56	77
MACY	F	15	66	112
PHILLIP	M	16	72	150
ROBERT	M	12	64	128
RONALD	M	15	67	133
THOMAS	M	11	57	85
WILLIAM	m	15	66	112

figure 1-1

A **data value** is a single measurement: one person's height, the number of calories in one brand of bread, the annual rainfall in one city.

Observations The information about each person—name, sex, age, height, and weight—makes up one **observation**. You interviewed nineteen students, so you have nineteen observations. Each row in figure 1-1 corresponds to an observation.

An **observation** is a set of data values for the same individual: physical measurements for one person, nutritional values in one brand of bread, weather measurements for one city in California.

Variables In figure 1-1 each kind of measurement forms a column: the values in each column make up a **variable**. The weight values you collected make up the weight variable, the height values form the height variable, and so on.

A **variable** is a set of data values for the same measurement: the heights of all the persons in a class, the numbers of calories in different brands of bread, the annual rainfalls for California cities.

Naming variables You give each variable a **variable name** that you will use in describing the variable to SAS. You call the weight values WEIGHT, the names NAME, the sex values SEX, and so on.

Choose a **name** for each variable: the name can contain from one to eight characters. It can contain numbers, but must begin with a letter. Examples of names: HEIGHT, CALORIES, RAINFALL.

Data sets or files Most collections of data are made up of many observations, each containing several variables. These collections are **data sets** or **files.**

All the height-weight values in figure 1-1 make up a data set. The data set has nineteen observations and five variables.

A **data set** or **file** is a collection of observations: the physical measurements of all the students in a class; nutritional values for different brands of breads; weather measurements of cities in California.

Getting data into a form the computer can read   Now you need to get your data values into a form that the computer can read. You might enter them at a terminal, putting the names in columns 1-10, the sex values in column 12, the ages in columns 14 and 15, the heights in columns 17 and 18, and the weights in columns 20-22.[1]

```
------------------------------------------------------------------------------
Command ===>                                                   Program Editor

00001 ALFRED      M 14 69 112
00002 ALICE       F 13 56  84
00003 BARBARA     F 14 62 102
00004 BERNADETTE  F 13 65  98
00005 HENRY       M 14 63 102
00006 JAMES       M 12 57  83
00007 JANE        F 12 59  84
00008 JANET       F 15 62 112
00009 JEFFREY     M 13 62  84
00010 JOHN        M 12 59  99
00011 JOYCE       F 11 51  50
00012 JUDY        F 14 64  90
00013 LOUISE      F 12 56  77
00014 MARY        F 15 66 112
00015 PHILIP      M 16 72 150
00016 ROBERT      M 12 64 128
00017 RONALD      M 15 67 133
00018 THOMAS      M 11 57  85
00019 WILLIAM     M 15 66 112
00020
00021
00022
00023
00024
00025
00026
00027
00028
00029
```

figure 1-2

You could simplify the task of keying the data by not worrying about the columns: just separate each value with a space.[2] SAS will be able to read your data if they are entered this way, although some other programs may not.

Now you are ready to decide what you want SAS to do for you.

What do you want the SAS System to do?

Before you can put together a SAS job, you need an idea of what you want SAS to do. Let's say that you want these results from SAS:

- you want SAS to print each data line as it is read (a *data line* is the same as a *data card*).
- you want SAS to print your data again after they have been organized into a SAS data set.
- you want to produce a graph of the data, with height on the vertical axis, weight on the horizontal axis. On this graph, you want an 'F' printed for points representing females' height-weight values, an 'M' printed for points representing males' height-weight values.

The SAS job

The SAS job shown in figure 1-3 will produce these results. Each typed line represents a line you enter at a computer terminal or a card you punch at a keypunch. (The horizontal lines have been drawn to separate parts of the job.)

Notice that this job consists of three kinds of lines:

- the data lines make up the large middle section
- the system commands come first; these commands tell the computer whose job this is and that you want to use SAS. See your computing center staff if you do not know how to write these commands.
- all the other lines are SAS statements; each ends with a semicolon (;).

figure 1-3

```
              SYSTEM COMMANDS
           DATA HTWT;
              INPUT NAME $ 1-10 SEX $ 12 AGE 14-15 HEIGHT 17-18 WEIGHT 20-22;
              LIST;
              CARDS;
           ALFRED     M 14 69 112
           ALICE      F 13 56  84
           BARBARA    F 14 62 102
           BERNADETTE F 13 65  98
           HENRY      M 14 63 102
           JAMES      M 12 57  83
           JANE       F 12 59  84
           JANET      F 15 62 112
           JEFFREY    M 13 62  84
           JOHN       M 12 59  99
           JOYCE      F 11 51  50
           JUDY       F 14 64  90
           LOUISE     F 12 56  77
           MARY       F 15 66 112
           PHILIP     M 16 72 150
           ROBERT     M 12 64 128
           RONALD     M 15 67 133
           THOMAS     M 11 57  85
           WILLIAM    M 15 66 112
           PROC PRINT;
           PROC PLOT;
              PLOT HEIGHT*WEIGHT=SEX;
```

Let's take a look at each SAS statement briefly:

DATA HTWT; The DATA statement tells SAS that you want to read some data and put them into a SAS data set named HTWT.

INPUT NAME $ 1-10 SEX $ 12 AGE 14-15 HEIGHT 17-18 WEIGHT 20-22; The INPUT statement tells SAS how the data values are arranged on the data lines, and what the variable names are. NAME comes first, then SEX, AGE, HEIGHT, and WEIGHT. The columns that each occupies on the data lines also appear. The dollar signs after NAME and SEX tell SAS, "These values contain alphabetic characters."

LIST; The LIST statement tells SAS to print the information on each data line as SAS reads it.

CARDS; The CARDS statement tells SAS that the data lines come next.

PROC PRINT; The PROC PRINT statement asks SAS to print the data values.

PROC PLOT; The PROC PLOT statement tells SAS that you want a plot of the data.

PLOT HEIGHT*WEIGHT = SEX; The PLOT statement gives SAS the details of the plot you want: HEIGHT should be on the vertical axis, WEIGHT on the horizontal and each observation's SEX value should represent the height-weight point for the observation.

After putting the job together, you submit it to the computer. (If you don't know how to do this, check with a consultant at your computer center.) SAS then reads your job and carries out the actions you requested, printing the results.

These results appear in figure 1-4.[3]

The output of the SAS job At the top of each page is the title "SAS." You will learn in Chapter 4 to substitute your own titles.

The first page is the SAS log. It shows your SAS statements, messages from SAS to you, and the list of the data lines you requested with the LIST statement.

The PROC PRINT statement produced the second page. Your data also appear here in an organized form, with each column labeled.

The third page contains the plot requested by the PROC PLOT and the PLOT statements. Note that HEIGHT is on the vertical axis, WEIGHT is on the horizontal axis, and the height-weight points for the observations are represented by 'M' and 'F'.

```
   1          SAS(R) LOG    OS SAS 5.XX           MVS/XA JOB EXAMPLE   STEP SAS

NOTE: COPYRIGHT (C) 1984 SAS INSTITUTE INC., CARY, N.C.  27511, U.S.A.
NOTE: THE JOB EXAMPLE HAS BEEN RUN UNDER RELEASE 5.XX OF SAS
      AT SAS INSTITUTE DATA CENTER (XXXXXXXX).

   1          DATA HTWT;
   2             INPUT NAME $ 1-10 SEX $ 12 AGE 14-15 HEIGHT 17-18 WEIGHT 20-22;
   3             LIST;
   4             CARDS;


RULE:        ----+----1----+----2----+----3----+----4----+----5----+----6----+----7

   5          ALFRED     M 14 69 112
   6          ALICE      F 13 56  84
   7          BARBARA    F 14 62 102
   8          BERNADETTE F 13 65  98
   9          HENRY      M 14 63 102
  10          JAMES      M 12 57  83
  11          JANE       F 12 59  84
  12          JANET      F 15 62 112
  13          JEFFREY    M 13 62  84
  14          JOHN       M 12 59  99
  15          JOYCE      F 11 51  50
  16          JUDY       F 14 64  90
  17          LOUISE     F 12 56  77
  18          MARY       F 15 66 112
  19          PHILIP     M 16 72 150
  20          ROBERT     M 12 64 128
  21          RONALD     M 15 67 133
  22          THOMAS     M 11 57  85
  23          WILLIAM    M 15 66 112
NOTE: DATA SET WORK.HTWT HAS 19 OBSERVATIONS AND 5 VARIABLES. 488 OBS/TRK.
NOTE: THE DATA STATEMENT USED 0.05 SECONDS AND 108K.

  24          ;
  25          PROC PRINT;
NOTE: THE PROCEDURE PRINT USED 0.08 SECONDS AND 308K
      AND PRINTED PAGE 1.

  26          PROC PLOT;
  27             PLOT HEIGHT*WEIGHT=SEX;
NOTE: THE PROCEDURE PLOT USED 0.10 SECONDS AND 304K
      AND PRINTED PAGE 2.
NOTE: SAS USED 308K MEMORY.

NOTE: SAS INSTITUTE INC.
      SAS CIRCLE
      PO BOX 8000
      CARY, N.C. 27511-8000
```

figure 1-4

SAS   1

OBS	NAME	SEX	AGE	HEIGHT	WEIGHT
1	ALFRED	M	14	69	112
2	ALICE	F	13	56	84
3	BARBARA	F	14	62	102
4	BERNADETTE	F	13	65	98
5	HENRY	M	14	63	102
6	JAMES	M	12	57	83
7	JANE	F	12	59	84
8	JANET	F	15	62	112
9	JEFFREY	M	13	62	84
10	JOHN	M	12	59	99
11	JOYCE	F	11	51	50
12	JUDY	F	14	64	90
13	LOUISE	F	12	56	77
14	MARY	F	15	66	112
15	PHILIP	M	16	72	150
16	ROBERT	M	12	64	128
17	RONALD	M	15	67	133
18	THOMAS	M	11	57	85
19	WILLIAM	M	15	66	112

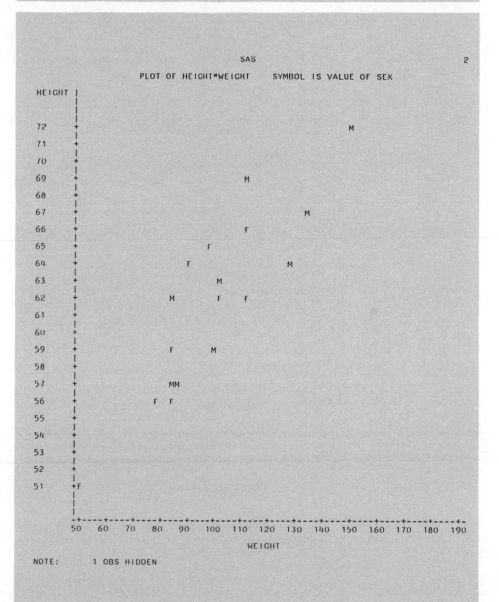

SAS   2

PLOT OF HEIGHT*WEIGHT   SYMBOL IS VALUE OF SEX

NOTE: 1 OBS HIDDEN

Using the SAS System: a summary

Now let's go over again the steps you took to get these results:

1. You collected the data and put them into a form that the computer could read.
2. You put together your SAS job.
3. You submitted the job to the computer, which ran the job and printed the results.

The rest of this book concentrates on step 2—putting together SAS jobs.

---

[1] You can enter data in many different ways. This illustration shows data that have been entered into the program editor screen of the SAS Display Manager. The display manager (described in *SAS User's Guide: Basics, Version 5 Edition*) is a useful part of base SAS software, but you do not have to use it to enter data or run SAS programs.

[2] If you enter your data this way, put a period in place of any value that is missing. See Chapter 2, "What happens if some data values are missing?"

[3] To make the output in this book a convenient size for reproduction, we used

OPTIONS LINESIZE=80;

as the first SAS statement in most of the jobs that produced the illustrations in chapters 1, 3, 6, and 8-13. If you recreate these jobs without this statement, your output will occupy more space on the page than the output shown here.

Chapter 2

Getting Your Data into a SAS® Data Set

The first step in most SAS jobs is to get your data into a SAS data set. This chapter tells you how to write the SAS statements that do this and begins with a brief discussion of SAS statements.

SAS statements SAS jobs are made up of SAS statements: SAS statements ask the SAS System to perform some activity.

The first word of a SAS statement tells SAS what activity you want to perform—creating a SAS data set, running a statistical procedure, printing a line of data.

In the rest of the SAS statement, you give SAS more information about how you want the activity performed—what to name the new data set, which procedure to run, how to arrange the line you want printed.

Every SAS statement ends with a semicolon.

For example, consider this SAS statement:

DATA HTWT;

The first word, DATA, tells SAS that you want to create a SAS data set. You give SAS more information with the word HTWT, which is the name you want SAS to give the data set. The statement ends with a semicolon.

> The first word in a SAS statement tells SAS what you want it to do—for example, **DATA** as the first word in a SAS statement tells SAS to create a SAS data set; **PROC** as the first word in a SAS statement tells SAS to run a SAS procedure.

> SAS statements contain information about how the activity should be performed—for example, what the new data set should be named, which SAS procedure to run.

> Every SAS statement ends with a semicolon.

You can put more than one SAS statement on a line. For example, the statements

DATA NEW;   could also be written
  INPUT X Y Z;   **DATA NEW; INPUT X Y Z; CARDS;**
  CARDS;

However, you may find it easier to understand your SAS jobs when each statement occupies one line.

SAS statements may begin in any column on a line. For clarity, the examples in this book show the DATA and PROC statements beginning in column 1; all other statements are indented.

Getting your data into a SAS data set

To get your data into a SAS data set, you need the SAS statements described in the rest of this chapter:

- the DATA statement
- the INPUT statement
- the CARDS or INFILE statement.

When you need to modify your data before you analyze them, you will also need the SAS statements described in the next chapter.

The DATA statement: beginning a SAS data set

The first statement in your SAS job is usually a DATA statement. You use the DATA statement to tell SAS that you want to create a SAS data set.

The DATA statement begins with the word DATA and then gives the name you choose for the data set you are creating:

DATA HTWT;

> The **DATA** statement begins creation of a SAS data set.

You can choose any name you want for the data set name, as long as it has eight or fewer characters and begins with a letter. You will find it easier to understand the statements in your SAS job if you choose names that describe the contents of the data sets.

You can leave out the data set name and write the DATA statement as simply

DATA;

Then SAS will give the data set a name.

Where to put the DATA statement Since the first step in a SAS job is usually to get the data into a SAS data set, a DATA statement is usually the first statement in a SAS job.

DATA HTWT;
  INPUT X 4–5 Y 8;
  CARDS;
data lines go here
PROC PRINT;

DATA statements may also appear in other places in SAS jobs when you create other SAS data sets.

The INPUT statment:
describing your data
to the SAS System

In the INPUT statement, you describe your data lines[1] to SAS.

Before you can write the INPUT statement, you must know what the information on your data lines represents. For example, to write the INPUT statement for the height-weight study, you need to know that columns 1–10 of each line contain the student's name, that column 12 contains the student's sex, that columns 14–15 contain the student's age, that columns 17–18 contain the student's height, and that columns 20–22 contain the student's weight.

The INPUT statement is important because SAS reads the data lines using the description you give. If this information is not correct, nothing that SAS does will produce correct results.

Where to put the INPUT statement The INPUT statement usually follows the DATA statement, making it the second statement in most jobs.

DATA HTWT;
  INPUT NAME $ 1–10;
  CARDS;
data lines go here
PROC PRINT;

How to write the INPUT statement The steps below use the height-weight study's data to show how to write an INPUT statement.

1. Begin with the word INPUT:
  INPUT
2. Choose a name for the first variable on your data lines. (Remember the naming rules: names must begin with letters and may have no more than 8 characters.) Write the name you choose:
  INPUT NAME

3. Is the variable character or numeric? If its values contain letters or other non-numeric characters, it's a character variable. If it is a character variable, put a dollar sign after the variable name.

INPUT NAME $

4. What columns do the variable values occupy on the data lines? Write the number of the column where the first data value begins, then write a dash, then the column where the data value ends:

INPUT NAME $ 1–10

It's important to give the entire range of columns where the variable's values might be found, even if not all the values occupy all the columns. For example, the first NAME value is ALFRED, which occupies only 6 columns. But another NAME value is BERNADETTE, which occupies all 10 columns.

If the data values for a variable occupy only one column on the data lines, put just the column's number:

INPUT NAME $ 1–10 SEX $ 12

5. If the variable is numeric, should it contain a decimal point that wasn't entered? If so, put a decimal point and the number of digits that should come after it;

INPUT GROWTH 26–28 .1;

This INPUT statement tells SAS to find the values of the variable GROWTH in columns 26, 27, and 28, and to put a decimal point before the last digit of each value if one isn't already there.

Repeat steps 2 through 5 for each variable that you want SAS to read. After you finish describing the data, put a semicolon to end the INPUT statement:

INPUT NAME $ 1–10 SEX $ 12 AGE 14–15 HEIGHT 17–18   WEIGHT 20–22;

This INPUT statement is now complete.

Special situations in the INPUT statement   The next five sections describe these special situations:

- you want to skip some of the data values on the input lines
- your INPUT statement is too long to fit on one line
- you have some missing data values
- the data values for each observation occupy more than one line
- you want to learn an easier way to write the INPUT statement.

You can read these five sections now, or you can skip directly to the section on the CARDS statement and finish this chapter.

Skipping data values   If your data lines contain values that you don't want SAS to read, don't describe these variables in the INPUT statement. SAS reads only the information you describe in the INPUT statement.

For example, if you needed only the NAME variable and the WEIGHT variable, you could use this INPUT statement:

INPUT NAME $ 1–10 WEIGHT 20–22;

Long INPUT statements If your INPUT statement is so long that you need more than one line to hold it, continue onto the next line. Don't split a variable name between two lines, though. When you use more than one line for an INPUT statement, your program will be easier to read if you indent the continuation line:

INPUT HEIGHT 23–27 WEIGHT 30–34 SEX $ 37 AGE 54–55
  NAME $ 60–70;

What happens if some data values are missing? Often one or more data values are missing. For example, suppose one of the students in the height-weight study was absent the day the heights and weights were recorded. You have the student's name, age, and sex, but not his height or weight.

If the columns that contain height and weight are blank on this student's data line, or if those columns contain periods, SAS treats that student's height and weight as **missing values**. Each SAS procedure has provisions for handling missing values. When SAS prints data values, it uses a period to indicate a missing value.

When data values for one observation occupy more than one card or line Since punched cards contain only 80 columns, it often takes more than one card to hold the data for an individual.

For example, here is the structure of some data where the variables for each observation take up three cards:

observation 1 $\begin{cases} \text{card 1} \\ \text{card 2} \\ \text{card 3} \end{cases}$

observation 2 $\begin{cases} \text{card 1} \\ \text{card 2} \\ \text{card 3} \end{cases}$

This situation occurs less often when the data values are on disk or tape, because the records holding the data can be longer than 80 columns.

When you write the INPUT statement for a set of data with several lines per observation, you need to let SAS know which variables are on which lines. The symbol # followed by a number tells SAS which line contains the next group of variables.

For example, the statement:

INPUT A 3–5 B 45–50 #2 X 10–11;

tells SAS to read variables A and B, then go to line 2 to read variable X.

When you're writing the INPUT statement and have described the variables on the first line, put a #2 to indicate that SAS should move to line 2 before reading any more variables. Then describe the variables on the second line. Continue in this manner if more lines are used for an observation.

You don't need to put a #1 before the first group of variables, because SAS automatically begins on the first line.

If you have more than one line per observation but don't need to read any variables from the last line in the set, let SAS know how many lines correspond to each observation by putting a # and the number of lines per observation at the end of the INPUT statement.

For example, if you have four lines per observation but need to read only from the first two lines, your INPUT statement might look like this:

INPUT A 3–5 B 45–50 #2 X 10–11 #4;

An easier way to write an INPUT statement You can simply list your variable names in the INPUT statement if your data values satisfy these conditions:

- each of the values on the data lines is separated from the next value by at least one blank column
- character variables have 8 characters or fewer
- the data don't include missing values, or else they are represented by periods
- numeric values include any necessary decimal points.

When your data values do meet these conditions, you can use these three steps to write your INPUT statement:

1. Begin with the word INPUT:

   INPUT

2. Choose a name for the first variable on your data lines, and write the name:

   INPUT NAME

3. If the variable is character, put a dollar sign ($) after the variable name:

   INPUT NAME $

Repeat steps 2 and 3 until you have listed all the variables. End the INPUT statement with a semicolon:

INPUT NAME $ SEX $ AGE HEIGHT WEIGHT;

When you write your INPUT statement this way, you must list all the variables on the input lines. It's not possible to skip any.

If your data are on terminal lines or cards: the CARDS statement

When you enter lines of data with your program at a terminal or on cards, the CARDS statement follows the DATA and INPUT statements in your SAS program. Its form is simply:

CARDS;

The CARDS statement tells SAS that the data lines come next. So put your data lines immediately after the CARDS statement.

DATA HTWT;
  INPUT NAME $ 1–10 SEX $ 12 AGE HEIGHT WEIGHT;
  CARDS;
data lines

If your data are on disk or tape: the INFILE statement

When your data values are on disk or tape, you must tell both SAS and the computer's operating system where to find the data.

To tell SAS where to find the data, your SAS program must include an INFILE statement. The INFILE statement contains a name called the fileref (short for file reference). For an example, an INFILE statement using the fileref STUDY is

INFILE STUDY;

Where to put the INFILE statement The INFILE statement goes before the INPUT statement that describes the data:

DATA HTWT;
  INFILE STUDY;
  INPUT NAME $ 1–10 SEX $ AGE HEIGHT WEIGHT;
PROC PRINT;

To tell the computer's operating system where to find the data, you must connect the fileref with the operating system's name for the location in which the data are stored. You must do this before the DATA statement that creates the SAS data set that uses the data lines. The way you make the connection depends on your operating system.[2]

Getting data into a SAS data set: a summary

1. Begin with a DATA statement.
2. Describe the arrangement of the data values with an INPUT statement.
3. If the data values are to be entered with the SAS program at the terminal or are on punched cards, use a CARDS statement next. Follow it with the data lines.
4. If the data values are on disk or tape, put an INFILE statement before the INPUT statement.

If you want to modify your data values before you use SAS procedures to analyze them, read the next chapter on modifying your data. If you are ready to begin analyzing the data, go to Chapter 4.

---

[1] In this book, the terms *card* and *line* mean the same thing; so do the terms *line* and *record*.

[2]   **AOS/VS, PRIMOS, and VMS:** Use a SAS FILENAME statement before the DATA statement. Here is a typical FILENAME statement for a data set on disk:

FILENAME STUDY *'minicomputerpathname'*;
DATA HTWT;
  INFILE STUDY;
  INPUT NAME $ 1–10 SEX $ AGE HEIGHT WEIGHT;
PROC PRINT;

Ask your computing center staff for the form of a minicomputer path name under your operating system.
   CMS and VM/PC: Use the fileref in a FILEDEF command before you begin the SAS session. Here is a typical FILEDEF command for a data set on disk:

FILEDEF STUDY DISK *filename filetype filemode*

Ask your computing center staff for the form of the filename, filetype, and filemode and any additional commands needed at your installation.
   OS: In a batch job, use the fileref in a DD statement in the job control language. Here is a typical DD statement for a data set on disk:

//STUDY DD DSN=*OSdatasetname*,DISP=SHR

Ask your computing center staff about the placement of the DD statement within the job control statements and any additional information needed at your installation.

In an interactive job (TSO), use the fileref in an ALLOCATE command before you begin the SAS session. Here is a typical ALLOCATE command for a data set on disk:

ALLOCATE FILE(STUDY) DATASET(*OSdatasetname*) SHR

Ask your computing center staff about any additional information needed at your installation.

VSE: Although most SAS names can contain up to eight characters, a fileref used under VSE can contain only seven characters.

In a batch job, use the fileref in a DLBL statement (or a TLBL statement, for a tape) in the control language for the job. Here are a typical DLBL, EXTENT, and ASSGN statement for a data set on disk:

```
// DLBL STUDY,'VSEdatasetname'
// EXTENT logicalunit,volumeserial
// ASSGN logicalunit,DISK,VOL=volumeserial,SHR
```

The INFILE statement must contain three options in addition to the fileref:

```
DATA HTWT;
   INFILE STUDY RECFM=recordformat BLKSIZE=blocksize LRECL=logicalrecordlength;
   INPUT NAME $ 1-10 SEX $ AGE HEIGHT WEIGHT;
PROC PRINT;
```

Ask your computing center staff about how to find the values of these options and any other information needed at your installation.

In an interactive job (ICCF), use the fileref in a /FILE statement in the ICCF proc that invokes the SAS System. Here is a typical /FILE statement for a data set on disk:

```
/FILE NAME=STUDY,ID='VSEdatasetname',UNITS=logicalunit
/ SERIAL=volumeserial
```

The INFILE statement must contain three options in addition to the fileref:

```
DATA HTWT;
   INFILE STUDY RECFM=recordformat BLKSIZE=blocksizeLRECL=logicalrecordlength;
      INPUT NAME $ 1-10 SEX $ AGE HEIGHT WEIGHT;
PROC PRINT;
```

Ask your computing center staff about how to find the values of these options and any other information needed at your installation.

Chapter 3

Getting Your Data in Shape

Data are often not in the shape you want when you get them. For example, consider the height-weight study from Chapter 1. You might want the students' weights in kilograms rather than in pounds. You can get weights in kilograms by using a SAS *program statement* to create a new variable containing the weight values in kilograms:

```
DATA HTWTKIL;
   INPUT NAME $ 1-10 SEX $ 12 AGE 14-15 HEIGHT 17-18
      WEIGHT 20-22;
   WTKILO = WEIGHT*.45;
   CARDS;
data lines go here
```

The shaded statement above creates a new variable called WTKILO by multiplying each weight value by .45. **Creating new variables**, below, explains how to write this statement.

What are SAS program statements?

You use some SAS program statements to work with the observations as they are read in—for example, to create new variables, to list data lines, to delete observations. Other program statements give SAS extra information about the data set you are creating. And still other program statements change the order in which SAS carries out program statements.

Program statements are *optional* in SAS jobs. You are not required to include them, and many SAS jobs consist simply of DATA, INPUT, and CARDS statements, followed by the data and then by PROC statements.

But as you tackle more challenging data analysis jobs, you will rely on program statements to help you tailor SAS programs to the requirements at hand.

Where to put program statements

Program statements go after the INPUT statement and before the CARDS statement:

DATA;
    INPUT NAME $ 1–10 SEX $ AGE HEIGHT WEIGHT;
    program statements go here
    CARDS;
data lines
PROC PRINT;

How the SAS System creates a data set

To understand how to use program statements, you first need to know how SAS creates a data set.

When SAS creates a data set, it goes through the steps below for *each* observation of your data:

1. SAS uses the description in the INPUT statement to read the observation.
2. SAS uses the data values in this observation to carry out any program statements that are present.
3. SAS adds the observation to the data set being created.

It is important to understand that program statements are carried out once for each observation. Take as an example the LIST statement in the SAS job shown in the first chapter. Its form is simply

LIST;

and it asks SAS to list the observation that has just been read.

Although the LIST statement appears only once in this job, it is carried out nineteen times, because there are nineteen observations.

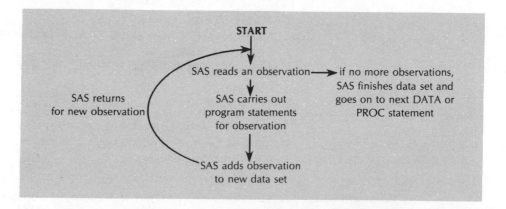

figure 3-1

Creating new variables

When you create a new variable, you add another set of data values to your data set. For example, suppose you create a new variable for the height-weight data set containing the students' weights in kilograms. Besides the name, sex, age, height, and weight for each student in your data set, you now also have each student's weight in kilograms.

OBS	NAME	SEX	AGE	HEIGHT	WEIGHT	WTKILO
1	ALFRED	M	14	69	112	50.40
2	ALICE	F	13	56	84	37.80
3	BARBARA	F	14	62	102	45.90
4	BERNADETTE	F	13	65	98	44.10
5	HENRY	M	14	63	102	45.90
6	JAMES	M	12	57	83	37.35
7	JANE	F	12	59	84	37.80
8	JANET	F	15	62	112	50.40
9	JEFFREY	M	13	62	84	37.80
10	JOHN	M	12	59	99	44.55
11	JOYCE	F	11	51	50	22.50
12	JUDY	F	14	64	90	40.50
13	LOUISE	F	12	56	77	34.65
14	MARY	F	15	66	112	50.40
15	PHILIP	M	16	72	150	67.50
16	ROBERT	M	12	64	128	57.60
17	RONALD	M	15	67	133	59.85
18	THOMAS	M	11	57	85	38.25
19	WILLIAM	M	15	66	112	50.40

figure 3-2

To create a new variable:

1. Choose a name for the new variable. For example, you might choose the name WTKILO for the new variable to contain the weight-in-kilograms values. Just as you use the name WEIGHT to refer to the weight-in-pounds values, you will use the name WTKILO to refer to the weight-in-kilograms values.
2. Figure out the formula necessary to create the variable. To create the WTKILO variable, for example, you need to know that one pound is .45 kilograms. You thus need to use the formula

   weight in kilograms = weight in pounds x .45 .

3. Write the formula as a SAS statement, putting the new variable name on the left side of the equal sign:

WTKILO = WEIGHT*.45;

This statement says to SAS

- for each observation in the data set, multiply the WEIGHT value by .45 (the * means *multiply* to SAS)
- make the result the WTKILO value for the observation.

SAS statements like the one above are called *assignment statements*, because they assign values to variables.

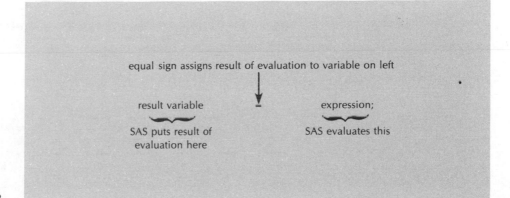

equal sign assigns result of evaluation to variable on left

result variable = expression;

SAS puts result of evaluation here   SAS evaluates this

figure 3-3

Modifying variables

You can also use an assignment statement to modify a variable that you already have in your data set. For example, suppose you wanted to have each student's height in feet instead of inches. Since you know that one foot contains 12 inches, you divide the number of inches by 12:

height in feet = height in inches divided by 12.

The corresponding SAS statement is

HEIGHT = HEIGHT/12;

This statement tells SAS to divide the old HEIGHT value in each observation by 12 (the / means *divide* in SAS) and to make the result the new HEIGHT value for that observation.

Statements like the one above *look* as though you are saying that height equals height divided by 12—a confusing impossibility. But the equal sign here means "assign the value on the right to the variable on the left."

Figure 3-4 shows the symbols to use in assignment statement calculations.

Symbol	Operation	Example	In SAS
**	Exponentiation	$Y \leftarrow X^2$	$Y = X^{**}2$
*	Multiplication	$A \leftarrow B \times C$	$A = B^*C$
/	Division	$G \leftarrow H \div I$	$G = H/I$
+	Addition	$R \leftarrow S + T$	$R = S + T$
−	Subtraction	$U \leftarrow V - X$	$U = V - X$

figure 3-4

IF statements

Sometimes you want SAS to carry out an action for certain observations in the data set, but not for all observations. For example, suppose you want to list just those input lines where the value of AGE is less than 14. You can use an IF statement to do this:

DATA YOUNG;
    INPUT NAME $ 1–10 SEX $ AGE HEIGHT WEIGHT;
    IF AGE LT 14 THEN LIST;
    CARDS;
data lines

As SAS reads each observation, it checks the AGE value. If the AGE value is less than 14, SAS carries out the LIST statement, printing the data line. When the AGE value is not less than 14, SAS ignores the LIST statement for that observation.

IF statements have this structure:

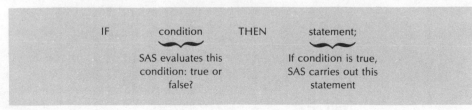

figure 3-5

For each observation, the IF condition is either *true* or *false*. For example, the IF condition AGE LT 14 is true for an observation where the AGE value is less than 14. It is false for observations where the AGE value is 14 or greater. When the IF condition is true, SAS carries out the statement after the THEN.

The IF condition can be a simple comparison of a variable and a value:

IF HEIGHT GT 72 THEN DELETE;

or a comparison of two variables

IF PRETEST LT TEST THEN IMPROVE = 'YES';
ELSE IMPROVE = 'NO';

The IF condition can involve several comparisons joined by ANDs and ORs:

IF AGE LT 13 AND HEIGHT GT 72 THEN LIST;
IF NAME = 'MARY' OR NAME = 'PHILIP' THEN LIST;
IF HEIGHT GE 60 OR WEIGHT GT 100 THEN LIST;

Figure 3-6 shows the operators you can use in IF conditions.[1]

symbol	abbreviation	comparison
<	LT	less than
<=	LE	less than or equal to
>	GT	greater than
>=	GE	greater than or equal to
=	EQ	equal to
¬=	NE	not equal to

comparison operators

figure 3-6

DELETE statements: getting rid of observations

When you want to discard certain observations, perhaps because you do not need them for your data analysis or because they contain invalid data, you can use the DELETE statement:

DELETE;

When this statement is carried out, SAS stops working on the current observation, does *not* add it to the SAS data set being created, and begins immediately on the next observation.

The DELETE statement normally appears as part of an IF statement:

IF SEX = 'M' THEN DELETE;

Then the IF condition (is the SEX value equal to 'M'?) is checked for each observation. When an observation meets the condition, SAS carries out the DELETE statement: SAS stops working on the observation, does not add it to the data set, and returns immediately for the next observation.

When the IF condition isn't true for an observation, SAS continues carrying out program statements for the observation and adds it to the data set being created before returning for the next observation.

LIST statements: getting the SAS System to print data lines

If you want SAS to print your data lines on the SAS log, use a LIST statement:

LIST;

SAS carries out the LIST statement by printing the current observation—the observation that has just been read—on the SAS log after the LIST statement.

Frequently, you only want to print an input line when one of the variables has a questionable value. In this situation, use LIST with an IF statement:

IF AGE <0 THEN LIST;

SAS checks each observation's AGE value. When the AGE value is less than 0, SAS prints the data line. When the AGE value is 0 or greater, SAS ignores the LIST statement.

Subsetting IF statements: selecting observations

Sometimes you want only certain observations included in the data set being created. For example, suppose that you want only females in the data set. You can use a subsetting IF statement to select just those observations where the SEX value is 'F':

IF SEX = 'F';

This statement means, "If the SEX value for an observation is 'F', add that observation to the data set. If the SEX value for an observation is not 'F', stop carrying out program statements for that observation and do not add it to the data set. Instead, return for the next observation."

The subsetting IF statement is exactly the reverse of the IF statement followed by a DELETE. It is just more straightforward and easier to write. These two statements have exactly the same effect:

IF SEX = 'F';

and

IF SEX NE 'F' THEN DELETE;

You might look at the subsetting IF statement as a turnstile that admits observations when the IF condition is true. Other observations cannot pass the turnstile.

---

[1] If the symbol ⌐ is not available on your terminal, use the symbol ∧ .

Chapter 4

Getting Answers:
How To Use SAS® Procedures

DATA and PROC steps   So far in this book you have learned to get your data into a SAS data set using

- a DATA statement to begin creating the SAS data set
- an INPUT statement to describe the data to the SAS System
- optional program statements to modify the data
- a CARDS statement to signal the beginning of the data lines or an INFILE statement to locate data values on disk or tape.

These statements together make up a **DATA step**, the part of a SAS job that creates a SAS data set.

> The statements that ask the SAS System to create a SAS data set make up a **DATA step.**

Once you have created a SAS data set, you're ready to use SAS procedures to analyze and process that data set. SAS **procedures** are computer programs that read your SAS data set, perform various computations, and print the results of the computations.

For example, the PRINT procedure reads your SAS data set, arranges the data values in an easy-to-read form, and prints them. The MEANS procedure reads your SAS data set, computes the mean and other descriptive statistics, and prints those statistics.

Some SAS procedures can also create SAS data sets containing the results of the computations. For example, the MEANS procedure can create a SAS data set containing means and other statistics.

> SAS **procedures** are computer programs that read your SAS data set, perform various computations, and print the results.

The statements that ask SAS to run a procedure make up a **PROC** (pronounced *prock*) step, the part of a SAS job that processes and analyzes a SAS data set.

> The statements that ask SAS to process or analyze a SAS data set make up a **PROC step**.

DATA and PROC steps get their names from the SAS statements DATA and PROC (short for PROCEDURE), which start off the steps. For example, this DATA step

DATA TEST;
  INPUT X Y Z;
  CARDS;
data lines

begins with a DATA statement and creates a SAS data set. This PROC step

PROC PLOT;
  PLOT Y*X;
  TITLE 'PLOT OF EXPERIMENTAL DATA';

begins with a PROC statement and processes a data set.

How you combine DATA and PROC steps to use the SAS System

You use the SAS System by stringing together DATA steps and PROC steps:

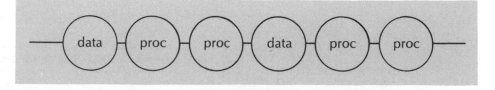

figure 4-1

Simple SAS jobs, like the ones you've seen so far in this book, usually consist of a DATA step followed by one or more PROC steps:

DATA TEST;
  INPUT X Y Z;
  CARDS;
data lines
PROC PLOT;
  PLOT Y*X;

Often, though, you want to work with more than one data set in a SAS job. For example, consider the height-weight study in the first part of this book. You might want to create a second data set containing last year's heights and weights for the students in your study. Then, after analyzing this year's and last year's data, you might merge these two data sets to form a third one.

DATA steps and PROC steps don't have to come in any special order. You can start with a DATA step, then use a PROC step, another PROC step, then a DATA step, and so on.

Once you create a SAS data set in a SAS job, that data set stays ready for you to use at any point in the job.

How to use PROC steps to get answers

The PROC step always begins with a PROC statement giving the name of the SAS procedure you want to run. For example, if you want to run the PRINT procedure, you begin the PROC step with the statement

PROC PRINT;

> PROC steps always begin with a PROC statement giving the name of the procedure that you want to run.

All SAS procedures for processing data[1] are alike in that you can tell the procedure

- what data set you want processed
- whether you want it processed in subsets
- which variables you want processed.

The most common situation

Most SAS procedures automatically handle the most common situation, where

- you want to process the most recently created SAS data set
- you want all the variables processed (or all the numeric variables, for a computational procedure)
- you want the entire data set processed at once, rather than in subsets.

Since SAS handles this situation automatically, much of the time your PROC step need only include a PROC statement giving the name of the procedure you want run. For example, the single statement

PROC PRINT;

is a PROC step that asks SAS to read the most recently created SAS data set, arrange all the variables in an easy-to-read form, and print them.

Combining a typical DATA step with this PROC step gives us this four-line SAS job:

DATA ONE;
   INPUT SEX $ AGE HEIGHT WEIGHT;
   CARDS;
data lines
PROC PRINT;

SAS procedures sometimes do require additional statements to give the procedure more information about what you want. For example, to use the PLOT procedure you must tell SAS what variable you want on the vertical axis and what variable on the horizontal axis:

PROC PLOT;
  PLOT HEIGHT*AGE;

This PROC step asks SAS to read the most recently created SAS data set and print a plot with the variable HEIGHT on the vertical axis versus the variable AGE on the horizontal axis. (The first variable mentioned in the PLOT statement goes on the vertical axis; the second variable mentioned is used on the horizontal axis.)

The individual procedure descriptions—PRINT, FREQ, MEANS, and so on—later in this book give complete information about when these additional statements are necessary.

Telling the PROC what data set you want processed

If you want the procedure to use the last data set you created, or if you have created only one data set, your PROC statement need give only the procedure name:

PROC PRINT;

When you want the procedure to use a data set that isn't the most recently created one, or when several data sets are created in the job and you want to minimize confusion, specify the name of the SAS data set you want processed after the word DATA followed by an equal sign:

PROC PRINT DATA = OLD;

This statement tells SAS to run the PRINT procedure using the data set OLD.

If you want to process a data set other than the most recently created one, give the name of the SAS data set you want processed after DATA= in the PROC statement:

PROC PRINT DATA = OLD;

Telling the PROC what variables you want processed

If you want the procedure to use all the variables in your SAS data set, you need do nothing, because the procedure automatically uses them all. (Some procedures automatically use all the numeric variables.)

But if you want to analyze only certain variables, you can use the VARIABLES statement (usually abbreviated to VAR) to give the names of these variables:

PROC MEANS;
  VAR HEIGHT WEIGHT;

The PROC statement tells SAS that you want to run the MEANS procedure on the most recently created data set. The VAR statement tells SAS that only the variables HEIGHT and WEIGHT are to be processed by the MEANS procedure.

> List the variables you want the procedure to process in a VAR statement:
>
> **PROC PRINT;**
> **VAR AGE HEIGHT;**

Do you want your data processed in subsets?

If you want your entire data set processed at once, SAS automatically handles it that way.

Often, however, you want your data processed in subsets. For example, you might want to run PROC MEANS first for the females in your study and then for the males.

You ask SAS to process data in subsets by putting a BY statement after the PROC statement. In the BY statement, give the variable (or variables) that define the subset. For example, to run the procedure first for females, then for males, you give the variable SEX in the BY statement:

PROC MEANS DATA = HTWT;
VAR HEIGHT WEIGHT;
BY SEX;

These statements ask SAS to:

- run the procedure MEANS on the data set HTWT
- use just the variables HEIGHT and WEIGHT for the analysis
- run the procedure first on the observations having an 'F' value for SEX, then on the observations having an 'M' value.

> To process data in subsets, list the variables that define those subsets in a BY statement:
>
> **PROC MEANS;**
> **BY RACE SEX;**

Before you can use a BY statement with a SAS procedure, you must make sure that the data set is arranged in the order of the BY variables. For example, before you can use the statement

BY SEX;

the observations must be arranged with those having a SEX value of 'F' (or 1, or whatever the values of SEX are) first, followed by those with a SEX value of 'M'.

If the data aren't in this order, use the SORT procedure to rearrange them. You can use the same BY statement with PROC SORT that you want to use with the other procedure. For example, to sort the data set containing the height-weight values in order of SEX, use the statements

PROC SORT DATA = HTWT;
BY SEX;

The SORT procedure reads the HTWT data set and rearranges it so that all the observations with a SEX value of 'F' are first, followed by the observations with a sex value of 'M'. Now you can use the statement

BY SEX;

after the PROC MEANS statement.

Before you can use a BY statement, the data must be sorted by the values of the variables in the BY statement.

---

[1] There are some SAS procedures that perform utility applications and do not process SAS data sets, but they aren't covered in this book.

Chapter 5

Rearranging Your Data Using PROC SORT

When do you need to sort your data?
What is sorting?
How to use PROC SORT
PROC SORT output

Since data are often recorded in random order they are usually still in this order when you're ready to analyze them with the SAS System. The data from a Wyoming questionnaire follow an Alabama questionnaire; Zeke's and Abby's data cards are next to each other; and observations for males and females are intermixed.

When do you need to sort your data?

The order of the data observations doesn't matter for much of the statistical processing you will do. For example, the mean height is the same number no matter what order the observations have.

Often, however, you do want the observations arranged in some definite order. For example, to check the questionnaire data for valid answers, you might want to print them by state of residence: all the Alabama answers, then all the Alaska answers, and so on. For the height-weight study, you might want to list the observations in alphabetical order by student name. Or you might want to look first at the females in your study, then at the males.

SAS often needs the observations in a data set to be in some definite order. For example, if you wanted to combine this year's height-weight information with last year's, both sets of data would need to have the same order—for example, alphabetical by name. And, as we discussed in Chapter 4, a data set must be sorted before you can use a BY statement to process it.

What is sorting?

Sorting is rearranging the observations in your data set into an order determined by the values of one or more variables.

Suppose you have a set of index cards with a book title and the author's name on each card. If you wanted the cards in order by the authors' names, you might put the cards into 26 stacks (one for each letter of the alphabet), and then put each stack in order. The cards would then be sorted by author's name.

If you next wanted the cards in order by the book titles, you would need to go through the entire process again, this time using the book titles for the alphabetizing.

In both these cases, you are sorting by one variable: the first sort is by author's name, and the second is by book title.

A different situation would be sorting questionnaires from a survey. First you put them in order by state. Next, for each state, you put the questionnaires in order by city. Finally, you alphabetize each city's questionnaires by the respondent's last name.

In this case, you are sorting by three variables—the state, the city, and the respondent's name.

How to use PROC SORT

To sort your data, use a PROC SORT statement followed by a BY statement that gives the variables by which you want to sort the data set.[1]

For example, these statements sort the height-weight data set by NAME:

PROC SORT DATA = HTWT;
   BY NAME;

If you want to sort a data set named SURVEY by state, then by city within state, and finally by name within city, you would use these statements:

PROC SORT DATA = SURVEY;
   BY STATE CITY NAME;

If you want sorted and unsorted versions of your data SAS normally reads the data set identified by DATA= in the PROC SORT statement (or the most recently created data set if DATA= is not used). SAS rearranges this data set in the order of the variables in the BY statement and writes the rearranged data set back out with the same data set name. The unsorted version of the data set disappears.

If you want to keep the unsorted version of the data set, specify OUT= in the PROC SORT statement to create another data set containing the sorted version:

PROC SORT DATA = OLD OUT = NEW;
   BY SEX;

Now you have two data sets, OLD and NEW. Data set NEW contains the same observations as data set OLD, but they are sorted by the values of the variable SEX.

PROC SORT output

PROC SORT doesn't print any procedure output, although it does print a report on the SAS log telling how much storage and time it used, and how many observations the sorted data set contains.

---

[1] Different computer operating systems may use different sorting sequences. If you run all your SAS programs under a single operating system, you do not need to worry about the sorting sequence. If you move SAS programs from one operating system to another, check with your computing center staff for information on sorting sequences.

Chapter 6

Printing Your Data Using PROC PRINT

The natural first step after getting your data into a SAS data set is to print it.

You want to verify that the data were read correctly. You want to check for keying errors. And you may see an obvious mistake that will alert you to other, not-so-obvious problems.

Printing your data also gives you a handy reference to the data values themselves—useful even when you're really interested in summarizing the data rather than looking at individual values.

Report writing: what's a report? When you use SAS software to ask the computer a question about your data, the SAS System prints your answer in the form of a *report*.

For example, you might ask the question, "What are the names of the females in the height-weight study? How about the males?" You use the SAS statements below and SAS prints your answers—a list of the females and a list of the males.

```
PROC PRINT DATA = HTWT;
  BY SEX;
```

What kind of questions can reports answer? You can use report writing to answer just about any question about your data that doesn't require a statistical test. Questions that involve checking each observation for certain values are easy to handle. Rearranging the data values—for example, printing alphabetical lists—is also easy. With a little work, you can also include totals and subtotals in your reports.

How to print your data

After you have used a DATA step to get your data values into a SAS data set, you can print the data values in an easy-to-read form with the statement

PROC PRINT;

Here is an example:

DATA HTWT;
  INPUT NAME $ 1-10 SEX $ AGE HEIGHT WEIGHT;
    CARDS;
data cards
PROC PRINT;

OBS	NAME	SEX	AGE	HEIGHT	WEIGHT
1	ALICE	F	13	56	84
2	BARBARA	F	14	62	102
3	BERNADETTE	F	13	65	98
4	JANE	F	12	59	84
5	JANET	F	15	62	112
6	JOYCE	F	11	51	50
7	JUDY	F	14	64	90
8	LOUISE	F	12	56	77
9	MARY	F	15	66	112
10	ALFRED	M	14	69	112
11	HENRY	M	14	63	102
12	JAMES	M	12	57	83
13	JEFFREY	M	13	62	84
14	JOHN	M	12	59	99
15	PHILIP	M	16	72	150
16	ROBERT	M	12	64	128
17	RONALD	M	15	67	133
18	THOMAS	M	11	57	85
19	WILLIAM	M	15	66	112

figure 6-1

Using just the PROC PRINT statement prints the most recently created SAS data set. If you want to print some other data set, you can specify DATA= in the PROC PRINT statement:

PROC PRINT DATA = OLD;

Adding titles to your report

You can put up to 10 titles on the pages of your report. For example, the statements

PROC PRINT;
  TITLE 'HEIGHT-WEIGHT STUDY';

produce this output:

HEIGHT-WEIGHT STUDY

OBS	NAME	SEX	AGE	HEIGHT	WEIGHT
1	ALICE	F	13	56	84
2	BARBARA	F	14	62	102
3	BERNADETTE	F	13	65	98
4	JANE	F	12	59	84
5	JANET	F	15	62	112
6	JOYCE	F	11	51	50
7	JUDY	F	14	64	90
8	LOUISE	F	12	56	77
9	MARY	F	15	66	112
10	ALFRED	M	14	69	112
11	HENRY	M	14	63	102
12	JAMES	M	12	57	83
13	JEFFREY	M	13	62	84
14	JOHN	M	12	59	99
15	PHILIP	M	16	72	150
16	ROBERT	M	12	64	128
17	RONALD	M	15	67	133
18	THOMAS	M	11	57	85
19	WILLIAM	M	15	66	112

figure 6-2

Or you can use several titles. In the job below, the TITLE goes on the first line, TITLE3 on the third line, and TITLE5 on the fifth line.

```
DATA HTWT1982;
   INPUT NAME $ 1-10 SEX $ AGE HEIGHT WEIGHT;
   CARDS;
data cards
PROC PRINT;
   TITLE 'HEIGHT-WEIGHT STUDY';
   TITLE3 '1982 SAMPLE';
   TITLE5 'LINCOLN SCHOOL, ROOM 241';
```

```
                    HEIGHT-WEIGHT STUDY

                       1982 SAMPLE

                  LINCOLN SCHOOL, ROOM 241

        OBS    NAME         SEX    AGE    HEIGHT    WEIGHT

          1    ALICE         F      13      56        84
          2    BARBARA       F      14      62       102
          3    BERNADETTE    F      13      65        98
          4    JANE          F      12      59        84
          5    JANET         F      15      62       112
          6    JOYCE         F      11      51        50
          7    JUDY          F      14      64        90
          8    LOUISE        F      12      56        77
          9    MARY          F      15      66       112
         10    ALFRED        M      14      69       112
         11    HENRY         M      14      63       102
         12    JAMES         M      12      57        83
         13    JEFFREY       M      13      62        84
         14    JOHN          M      12      59        99
         15    PHILIP        M      16      72       150
         16    ROBERT        M      12      64       128
         17    RONALD        M      15      67       133
         18    THOMAS        M      11      57        85
         19    WILLIAM       M      15      66       112
```

figure 6-3

Printing subsets of your data

When your data include several different groups, you can print a separate list for each group. For example, these statements first print the data for females and then the data for males:

```
PROC PRINT;
   BY SEX;
```

```
------------------------------- SEX=F -------------------------------

        OBS    NAME         AGE    HEIGHT    WEIGHT

          1    ALICE         13      56        84
          2    BARBARA       14      62       102
          3    BERNADETTE    13      65        98
          4    JANE          12      59        84
          5    JANET         15      62       112
          6    JOYCE         11      51        50
          7    JUDY          14      64        90
          8    LOUISE        12      56        77
          9    MARY          15      66       112


------------------------------- SEX=M -------------------------------

        OBS    NAME         AGE    HEIGHT    WEIGHT

         10    ALFRED        14      69       112
         11    HENRY         14      63       102
         12    JAMES         12      57        83
         13    JEFFREY       13      62        84
         14    JOHN          12      59        99
         15    PHILIP        16      72       150
         16    ROBERT        12      64       128
         17    RONALD        15      67       133
         18    THOMAS        11      57        85
         19    WILLIAM       15      66       112
```

figure 6-4

Printing Your Data Using PROC PRINT   33

Remember that before you can use a BY statement (with PROC PRINT or with any other SAS procedure), the data set must already be sorted by the variables in the BY statement. So you may need to use a PROC SORT statement before the PROC PRINT statement:

PROC SORT;
  BY SEX;
PROC PRINT;
  BY SEX;

You can break your data down into smaller subsets by using two or more variables in the BY statement. For example, you could print a list of 14-year-old females, 14-year-old males, 15-year-old females, and so on:

PROC SORT;
  BY AGE SEX;
PROC PRINT;
  BY AGE SEX;

You can combine BY statements and TITLE statements. It doesn't matter whether the TITLE statements go before or after the BY statement:

PROC PRINT;
  BY AGE SEX;
  TITLE 'HEIGHT-WEIGHT STUDY';

Listing the variables in the order you want

So far, we've printed all the variables in the same order they had in the data set.

You can select only certain variables to be printed and ask that they be printed in a certain order by using the VAR (short for VARIABLES) statement. For example, the statements

PROC PRINT;
  VAR NAME AGE SEX HEIGHT;

ask SAS to print just the NAME, AGE, SEX, and HEIGHT variables in that order.

OBS	NAME	AGE	SEX	HEIGHT
1	ALICE	13	F	56
2	BARBARA	14	F	62
3	BERNADETTE	13	F	65
4	JANE	12	F	59
5	JANET	15	F	62
6	JOYCE	11	F	51
7	JUDY	14	F	64
8	LOUISE	12	F	56
9	MARY	15	F	66
10	ALFRED	14	M	69
11	HENRY	14	M	63
12	JAMES	12	M	57
13	JEFFREY	13	M	62
14	JOHN	12	M	59
15	PHILIP	16	M	72
16	ROBERT	12	M	64
17	RONALD	15	M	67
18	THOMAS	11	M	57
19	WILLIAM	15	M	66

figure 6-5

You can combine the VAR statement with the other PROC information statements, and it can appear anywhere:

PROC PRINT;
  VAR HEIGHT;
  BY AGE SEX;
  TITLE 'HEIGHT-WEIGHT STUDY';

Fancier reports   You can combine a simple DATA step with PROC PRINT to produce many kinds of reports.

For example, suppose you wanted to print a list of those students who weigh under 100 pounds. What you need to do is create a SAS data set containing just the observations for students weighing under 100 pounds, and then print that data set.

The SET statement   **Creating a SAS data set from another SAS data set**   Until now, we've used an INPUT statement to describe data. All the input data have come from punched cards, from lines entered at a terminal, or from disk or tape.

But your data can also come from a SAS data set that already exists. You can create another SAS data set using the observations from an existing data set.

To do this, use the word SET in place of the INPUT and CARDS (or INPUT and INFILE) statements:

DATA HTWT2;
  SET HTWT;

The DATA statement tells SAS to begin creating a SAS data set, as usual. The SET statement asks SAS to get the data from the existing SAS data set HTWT.

These two statements alone create a data set that is an exact copy of the data set HTWT.

Usually, there's not much sense in making an exact copy of a data set. So you use a subsetting IF statement to select just the observations you need. For example, to create a SAS data set containing just the observations with WEIGHT values under 100, use these statements:

DATA LIGHT;
  SET HTWT;
  IF WEIGHT<100;

The new data set LIGHT contains just those observations from data set HTWT where the WEIGHT value was less than 100.

Now you use a PROC PRINT statement to list those observations.

DATA LIGHT;
  SET HTWT;
  IF WEIGHT<100;
PROC PRINT;

OBS	NAME	SEX	AGE	HEIGHT	WEIGHT
1	ALICE	F	13	56	84
2	BERNADETTE	F	13	65	98
3	JANE	F	12	59	84
4	JOYCE	F	11	51	50
5	JUDY	F	14	64	90
6	LOUISE	F	12	56	77
7	JAMES	M	12	57	83
8	JEFFREY	M	13	62	84
9	JOHN	M	12	59	99
10	THOMAS	M	11	57	85

figure 6-6

You can add more PROC information statements after PROC PRINT to make the report look nicer: for example, a title explaining what the list represents:

DATA LIGHT;
  SET HTWT;
  IF WEIGHT<100;
PROC PRINT;
  TITLE 'STUDENTS WEIGHING UNDER 100 POUNDS';

The subsetting IF statement can get as complicated as you like. For example, to print a list of all 16-year-old males who weigh over 200 pounds, you could use these statements:

DATA HEAVY;
  SET HTWT;
  IF AGE = 16 AND SEX = 'M' AND WEIGHT>200;
PROC PRINT;

Chapter 7

Picturing Your Data Using PROC CHART and PROC PLOT

Printing columns of numbers gives you the exact values represented by your data, but it doesn't give you a clear picture of your data—where they peak, where the numbers begin to rise slowly, where the isolated values are.

The impact of a histogram or graph is direct. Compare these numbers and this picture:[1]

YEAR	SALES
1979	124835
1980	154119
1981	132087
1982	156218
1983	172376

figure 7-1

```
                           BAR CHART OF SALES
   SALES
         |                                                          *****
         |                                                          *****
         |                         *****              *****         *****
  150000 +                         *****              *****         *****
         |                         *****              *****         *****
         |                         *****              *****         *****
         |              *****       *****    *****     *****         *****
  120000 +              *****       *****    *****     *****         *****
         |              *****       *****    *****     *****         *****
         |              *****       *****    *****     *****         *****
         |              *****       *****    *****     *****         *****
   90000 +              *****       *****    *****     *****         *****
         |              *****       *****    *****     *****         *****
         |              *****       *****    *****     *****         *****
         |              *****       *****    *****     *****         *****
   60000 +              *****       *****    *****     *****         *****
         |              *****       *****    *****     *****         *****
         |              *****       *****    *****     *****         *****
         |              *****       *****    *****     *****         *****
   30000 +              *****       *****    *****     *****         *****
         |              *****       *****    *****     *****         *****
         |              *****       *****    *****     *****         *****
         |              *****       *****    *****     *****         *****
          -------------------------------------------------------------------
                       1979       1980     1981      1982          1983
                                          YEAR
```

figure 7-2

You see immediately exactly where the numbers go up, and how much they go up compared to the years before and after. This immediate impact is important when you have quantities of data to work with.

What bar charts show

Bar charts show the distribution of variable values. A bar chart might show the distribution of one variable's values; for example, you can compare the number of males and females in the height-weight study group by using the statements:

PROC CHART;
  VBAR SEX;

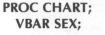

figure 7-3

```
                    FREQUENCY BAR CHART

          FREQUENCY

             10 +                           *****
                |                           *****
              9 +               *****       *****
                |               *****       *****
              8 +               *****       *****
                |               *****       *****
              7 +               *****       *****
                |               *****       *****
              6 +               *****       *****
                |               *****       *****
              5 +               *****       *****
                |               *****       *****
              4 +               *****       *****
                |               *****       *****
              3 +               *****       *****
                |               *****       *****
              2 +               *****       *****
                |               *****       *****
              1 +               *****       *****
                |               *****       *****
                ----------------------------------------
                                  F           M

                                    SEX
```

Bar charts can also show the relationship between two or more variables. For example, you can compare sales for each of the last three years using these statements to produce this chart:

PROC CHART;
  VBAR YEAR / SUMVAR = SALES DISCRETE;

```
              DEPARTMENT SALES FOR THE YEARS 1981-1983

                     BAR CHART OF SALES

        SALES
       40000 +                               *****
             |                               *****
             |                   *****       *****
             |                   *****       *****
             |                   *****       *****
       30000 +                   *****       *****
             |                   *****       *****
             |       *****       *****       *****
             |       *****       *****       *****
             |       *****       *****       *****
       20000 +       *****       *****       *****
             |       *****       *****       *****
             |       *****       *****       *****
             |       *****       *****       *****
             |       *****       *****       *****
       10000 +       *****       *****       *****
             |       *****       *****       *****
             |       *****       *****       *****
             |       *****       *****       *****
             ----------------------------------------
                     1981        1982        1983

                              YEAR
```

figure 7-4

<table>
<tr><td>**How to use
PROC CHART**</td><td>To get a vertical bar chart, follow the PROC CHART statement with a VBAR statement giving the variable whose distribution you want to see:</td></tr>
</table>

PROC CHART;
  VBAR SEX;

To get a horizontal bar chart, follow the PROC CHART statement with an HBAR statement giving the variable name:

PROC CHART;
  HBAR SEX;

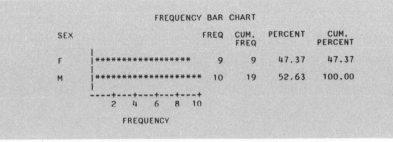

figure 7-5

**Showing relationships
between two variables
with PROC CHART**

One way to show two-variable relationships is with side-by-side charts. For example, to show the different percentages of males and females in this year's and last year's study, use these statements:

PROC CHART;
  VBAR SEX / GROUP = YEAR;

```
                            FREQUENCY BAR CHART
      FREQUENCY
                                                             *****
          5 +                                                *****
            |                                                *****
            |                                                *****
            |                                                *****
          4 +            *****                                *****
            |            *****                                *****
            |            *****                                *****
            |            *****                                *****
            |            *****                                *****
          3 +            *****                *****           *****
            |            *****                *****           *****
            |            *****                *****           *****
            |            *****                *****           *****
            |            *****                *****           *****
          2 +            *****      *****     *****           *****
            |            *****      *****     *****           *****
            |            *****      *****     *****           *****
            |            *****      *****     *****           *****
            |            *****      *****     *****           *****
          1 +            *****      *****     *****           *****
            |            *****      *****     *****           *****
            |            *****      *****     *****           *****
            |            *****      *****     *****           *****
            |            *****      *****.    *****           *****
            ------------------------------------------------------------
                          F          M         F              M    SEX

                       |----- 1981 ----|    |----- 1982 ----|  YEAR
```

figure 7-6

Side-by-side charts are most effective when the variable that the GROUP= option specifies has only a few values. Otherwise, you get many side-by-side charts, making it hard to compare them all.

Charts broken down by another variable

You can also show two-variable relationships by breaking down the sum of one variable by another variable. For example, you can show total sales broken down by department:

PROC CHART;
  VBAR DEPT / SUMVAR = SALES;

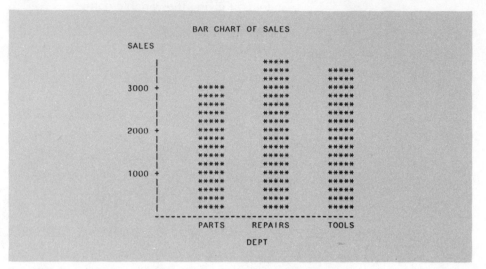

figure 7-7

Charts with subdivided bars

Still another way of showing two-variable relationships is to subdivide the bars to show the contribution of different kinds of observations to a total value. For example, you can show the count of males and females in each department by using the statements:

PROC CHART;
  VBAR DEPT / SUBGROUP = SEX;

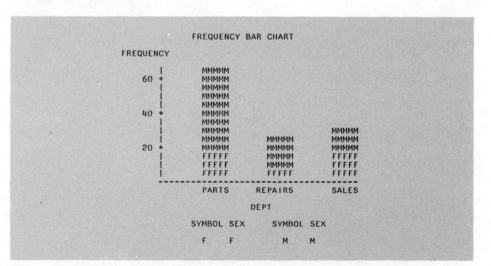

figure 7-8

You can also combine the GROUP= and SUBGROUP= options to show relationships among three variables. For example, you can show the counts of males and females in each department over the past two years by using the statements:

```
PROC CHART;
  VBAR DEPT / SUBGROUP = SEX  GROUP = YEAR;
```

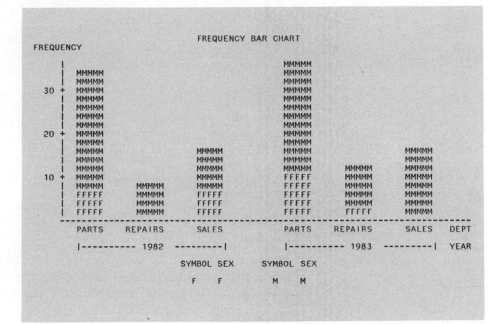

figure 7-9

<table>
<tr><td></td><td>**Producing charts for subgroups of the data**</td><td>When you want to run PROC CHART first for one group of observations and then for another, you can use a BY statement giving the variable that defines the groups. For example, to produce a chart first for the females in your study and then for the males, you could use these statements:</td></tr>
</table>

**Producing charts
for subgroups
of the data**

When you want to run PROC CHART first for one group of observations and then for another, you can use a BY statement giving the variable that defines the groups. For example, to produce a chart first for the females in your study and then for the males, you could use these statements:

```
PROC CHART;
  VBAR HEIGHT;
  BY SEX;
```

However, the GROUP=, SUBGROUP=, and SUMVAR= options described above are also useful in displaying the relationships between groups of your data.

What plotting is

When you plot two variables against each other, you first choose one variable for the vertical axis and the other for the horizontal axis. For example, suppose you want to plot height against weight for a set of observations. You choose height for the vertical axis, weight for the horizontal axis. Then, for each observation, you mark the point on the graph that corresponds to the HEIGHT and WEIGHT values in that observation.

SAS follows this same procedure in the PLOT procedure. For example, these statements produce a plot of HEIGHT against WEIGHT:

```
PROC PLOT;
  PLOT HEIGHT*WEIGHT;
```

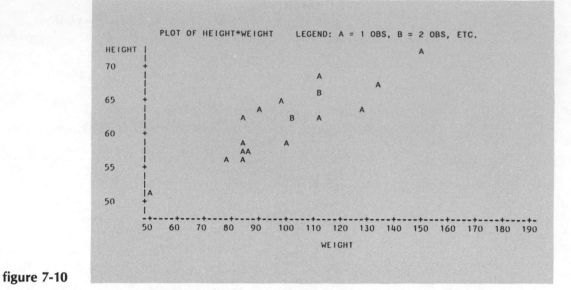

figure 7-10

How to use PROC PLOT   Follow the PROC PLOT statement with a PLOT statement giving the plots you want. For each plot, give first the variable you want on the vertical axis, then an asterisk (*), then the horizontal variable. The statements

PROC PLOT;
  PLOT Y*X;

produce a plot with Y on the vertical axis, X on the horizontal axis.

SAS prints one or both of these messages if it is unable to plot the value of a given observation:

NOTE: __ OBS HAD MISSING VALUES   __ OBS HIDDEN

Requesting several plots   You can request as many plots as you like in the PLOT statement. For example, these statements ask for two plots:

PROC PLOT;
  PLOT HEIGHT*AGE   WEIGHT*AGE;

Getting plots for subsets of your data   As with all SAS procedures for processing data, you can run the PLOT procedure on subsets of your data with the BY statement. For example, to graph HEIGHT vs. WEIGHT first for the females and then for the males in your data set, use the statements:

PROC PLOT;
  PLOT HEIGHT*WEIGHT;
  BY SEX;

These statements produce two separate plots, one for females and one for males.

(Remember to sort your data by SEX before using the BY statement with PROC PLOT.)

---

[1] To make the output in this chapter a convenient size for reproduction, we used

OPTIONS LINESIZE=64 PAGESIZE=40;

as the first SAS statement in most of the jobs that produced these illustrations. For 7-9 we used

OPTIONS LINESIZE=80 PAGESIZE=40;

and for 7-10 we used

OPTIONS LINESIZE=80 PAGESIZE=30;

If you recreate these jobs without one of these statements, your output will occupy more space on the page than the output shown here.

Frequencies and Crosstabulations Using PROC FREQ

What kind of variables are frequencies useful for?
How to get frequencies
How to get crosstabulations
How PROC FREQ treats missing values

Frequency tables may be a good way to summarize your data. Frequency tables show the distribution of a variable's values: you see at a glance how many observations in the data set have a given value. For example, say you want to know how many 12-year-olds were in the height-weight study, how many 13-year-olds, and so on. You can use PROC FREQ to find how many observations have an AGE value of 12, how many have an AGE value of 13, and so on:

PROC FREQ;
  TABLES AGE;

AGE	FREQUENCY	PERCENT	CUMULATIVE FREQUENCY	CUMULATIVE PERCENT
11	2	10.5	2	10.5
12	5	26.3	7	36.8
13	3	15.8	10	52.6
14	4	21.1	14	73.7
15	4	21.1	18	94.7
16	1	5.3	19	100.0

figure 8-1

You can break the data down further with crosstabulation tables, which show the joint distribution of two variables' values. For example, say you want to know how many 12-year-old females are in the height-weight data, how many 12-year-old males, how many 13-year-old females, and so on. You use the two variables AGE and SEX in the TABLES statement to find how many observations have an AGE value of 12 and SEX value of 'M', and so on:

PROC FREQ;
  TABLES AGE*SEX;

```
                        TABLE OF AGE BY SEX

              AGE         SEX

              FREQUENCY|
              PERCENT  |
              ROW PCT  |
              COL PCT  |F       |M       |   TOTAL
              ---------+--------+--------+
                    11 |      1 |      1 |      2
                       |   5.26 |   5.26 |  10.53
                       |  50.00 |  50.00 |
                       |  11.11 |  10.00 |
              ---------+--------+--------+
                    12 |      2 |      3 |      5
                       |  10.53 |  15.79 |  26.32
                       |  40.00 |  60.00 |
                       |  22.22 |  30.00 |
              ---------+--------+--------+
                    13 |      2 |      1 |      3
                       |  10.53 |   5.26 |  15.79
                       |  66.67 |  33.33 |
                       |  22.22 |  10.00 |
              ---------+--------+--------+
                    14 |      2 |      2 |      4
                       |  10.53 |  10.53 |  21.05
                       |  50.00 |  50.00 |
                       |  22.22 |  20.00 |
              ---------+--------+--------+
                    15 |      2 |      2 |      4
                       |  10.53 |  10.53 |  21.05
                       |  50.00 |  50.00 |
                       |  22.22 |  20.00 |
              ---------+--------+--------+
                    16 |      0 |      1 |      1
                       |   0.00 |   5.26 |   5.26
                       |   0.00 | 100.00 |
                       |   0.00 |  10.00 |
              ---------+--------+--------+
              TOTAL           9       10       19
                          47.37    52.63   100.00
```

figure 8-2

Crosstabulation tables can also show the distribution of values for three or more variables.

What kind of variables are frequencies useful for?

Frequencies and crosstabulations are useful mainly for *discrete* variables, those that have several distinct values. For example, the variable AGE in the height-weight study has six values; SEX has two values. Getting frequencies for AGE and SEX would give you useful information.

However, variables like WEIGHT have many values. For these continuous variables, statistics like the mean and standard deviation are more useful.

Another benefit of frequencies and crosstabulations: you can summarize character variables. Only numeric variables can be summarized by statistics like the mean and standard deviation.

How to get frequencies

To get frequency tables for all the variables in the most recently created data set, use just a PROC FREQ statement:

PROC FREQ;

If you want to use another data set, use DATA= in the PROC FREQ statement:

PROC FREQ DATA = OLD;

There is little purpose in getting frequency tables for variables like NAME that have many values. Thus, you will usually ask SAS to print frequencies for only selected variables in your data set. Give their names in a TABLES statement after the PROC FREQ statement:

PROC FREQ;
  TABLES AGE SEX;

How to get crosstabulations

To get a crosstabulation table, follow the PROC FREQ statement with a TABLES statement. Put the variable you want down the side of the table first, then an asterisk (*), then the variable you want across the top:

PROC FREQ;
  TABLES AGE*SEX;

You can ask for as many tables in one TABLES statement as you like. For example, the statements

PROC FREQ;
  TABLES SEX*RACE AGE*SEX RACE*RELIGION;

produce three crosstabulation tables.

To crosstabulate three variables, connect all three variable names with asterisks:

PROC FREQ;
  TABLES AGE*SEX*RACE;

A two-way crosstabulation table of the second and third variables is produced for each value of the first variable.

How PROC FREQ treats missing values

Missing values for variables appear in frequency and crosstabulation tables like other values. However, PROC FREQ does not include missing values when it calculates the percentages for row, column, and totals, unless the MISSING option is specified.

Chapter 9

Summarizing Your Data
with PROC MEANS

How to use PROC MEANS
Statistics you get automatically
Selecting statistics
Getting subset means
How PROC MEANS handles missing values

One goal of data analysis is to summarize the data.

For example, there are nineteen weight values in the height-weight study. You can get a complete picture of these weights by listing them all. But this means that you have to look at nineteen numbers. You can summarize these nineteen numbers by using PROC MEANS to compute the mean, or average. Then you have just one number that represents all nineteen.

PROC MEANS also finds other summary statistics, including the sum, the number of observations, the minimum, and the maximum.

How to use
PROC MEANS

To get summary statistics for all the numeric variables in the last data set created, use the PROC MEANS statement alone:

PROC MEANS;

VARIABLE	N	MEAN	STANDARD DEVIATION	MINIMUM VALUE	MAXIMUM VALUE	STD ERROR OF MEAN
AGE	19	13.31578947	1.49267216	11.00000000	16.0000000	0.34244248
HEIGHT	19	61.94736842	5.19052218	51.00000000	72.0000000	1.19078745
WEIGHT	19	99.84210526	22.81876216	50.00000000	150.0000000	5.23498307

figure 9-1

To get summary statistics for another data set, use DATA= in the PROC MEANS statement:

PROC MEANS DATA = YR1981;

To get summary statistics from some, but not all, numeric variables in the data set, list the variables you want in a VAR statement:

PROC MEANS;
   VAR HEIGHT WEIGHT;

Statistics you get automatically

PROC MEANS automatically prints the number of observations, the mean, the standard deviation, the minimum, and the maximum for each numeric variable. If the computer paper is wide enough, it also prints the variable label, the standard error of the mean, the sum, the variance, and the coefficient of variation.

Selecting statistics

You can ask SAS to print only the summary statistics you need. Corresponding to each PROC MEANS statistic is a keyword, as shown in the table below. In the PROC MEANS statement, give the keyword for each statistic you want.

Here are some of the keywords you can use in the PROC MEANS statement. When you use one or more of them, only the statistics you request are printed.

If you put this word in the PROC MEANS statement	you get this statistic
N	number of observations with non-missing value for the variable
NMISS	number of observations with missing value for the variable
MEAN	the mean or average
STD	the standard deviation
MIN	the minimum
MAX	the maximum
RANGE	the difference between the smallest and largest values
SUM	the sum of all the non-missing values of the variable

For example, if you wanted to see only the number of observations and sum of your numeric variables, include the keywords N and SUM in the PROC MEANS statement:

PROC MEANS N SUM;

```
                    VARIABLE              N        SUM

                    AGE                  19     253.00000000
                    HEIGHT               19    1177.00000000
                    WEIGHT               19    1897.00000000
```

figure 9-2

Getting subset means   You can get summary statistics for subsets of your data with PROC MEANS and a BY statement. For example, say you wanted to get the mean WEIGHT first for females and then for males. You would use a BY SEX statement with PROC MEANS:

PROC MEANS;
  BY SEX;
  VAR WEIGHT;

```
VARIABLE      N      MEAN     STANDARD     MINIMUM      MAXIMUM    STD ERROR
                              DEVIATION     VALUE        VALUE      OF MEAN

-------------------------------------- SEX=F --------------------------------------

WEIGHT        9  89.88888889  19.41934888  50.00000000  112.0000000  6.47311629

-------------------------------------- SEX=M --------------------------------------

WEIGHT       10  108.8000000  22.75863694  83.00000000  150.0000000  7.19691292
```

figure 9-3

Remember that before you can use a BY statement with any SAS procedure, the data set must already be sorted in the order of the variables in the BY statement. So you may need to use PROC SORT before you use PROC MEANS with a BY statement:

PROC SORT;
  BY SEX;
PROC MEANS;
  BY SEX;

You can break down the subsets further by using two or more variables in the BY statement. For example, to find the mean WEIGHT for each AGE-SEX subgroup, use both AGE and SEX in the BY statement:

PROC MEANS;
  BY AGE SEX;

VARIABLE	N	MEAN	STANDARD DEVIATION	MINIMUM VALUE	MAXIMUM VALUE	STD ERROR OF MEAN
------------------------------ AGE=11 SEX=F ------------------------------						
HEIGHT	1	51.00000000	.	51.00000000	51.00000000	.
WEIGHT	1	50.00000000	.	50.00000000	50.00000000	.
------------------------------ AGE=11 SEX=M ------------------------------						
HEIGHT	1	57.00000000	.	57.00000000	57.00000000	.
WEIGHT	1	85.00000000	.	85.00000000	85.00000000	.
------------------------------ AGE=12 SEX=F ------------------------------						
HEIGHT	2	57.50000000	2.12132034	56.00000000	59.00000000	1.50000000
WEIGHT	2	80.50000000	4.94974747	77.00000000	84.00000000	3.50000000
------------------------------ AGE=12 SEX=M ------------------------------						
HEIGHT	3	60.0000000	3.60555128	57.00000000	64.0000000	2.0816660
WEIGHT	3	103.3333333	22.81081615	83.00000000	128.0000000	13.1698308
------------------------------ AGE=13 SEX=F ------------------------------						
HEIGHT	2	60.50000000	6.36396103	56.00000000	65.00000000	4.50000000
WEIGHT	2	91.00000000	9.89949494	84.00000000	98.00000000	7.00000000
------------------------------ AGE=13 SEX=M ------------------------------						
HEIGHT	1	62.00000000	.	62.00000000	62.00000000	.
WEIGHT	1	84.00000000	.	84.00000000	84.00000000	.
------------------------------ AGE=14 SEX=F ------------------------------						
HEIGHT	2	63.00000000	1.41421356	62.00000000	64.0000000	1.00000000
WEIGHT	2	96.00000000	8.48528137	90.00000000	102.0000000	6.00000000
------------------------------ AGE=14 SEX=M ------------------------------						
HEIGHT	2	66.0000000	4.24264069	63.0000000	69.0000000	3.00000000
WEIGHT	2	107.0000000	7.07106781	102.0000000	112.0000000	5.00000000
------------------------------ AGE=15 SEX=F ------------------------------						
HEIGHT	2	64.0000000	2.82842712	62.0000000	66.0000000	2.00000000
WEIGHT	2	112.0000000	0.00000000	112.0000000	112.0000000	0.00000000
------------------------------ AGE=15 SEX=M ------------------------------						
HEIGHT	2	66.5000000	0.70710678	66.0000000	67.0000000	0.5000000
WEIGHT	2	122.5000000	14.84924240	112.0000000	133.0000000	10.5000000
------------------------------ AGE=16 SEX=M ------------------------------						
HEIGHT	1	72.0000000	.	72.0000000	72.0000000	.
WEIGHT	1	150.0000000	.	150.0000000	150.0000000	.

figure 9-4

How PROC MEANS handles missing values

Missing values are not included in any calculations that PROC MEANS does. For example, say a data set contained 20 observations and that two observations had missing values for the variable HEIGHT. All statistics for HEIGHT would be calculated from the 18 observations with non-missing HEIGHT values. If another variable, AGE, had no missing values, all 20 observations would be used to calculate statistics for AGE.

Chapter 10

Getting Correlations Using PROC CORR

What does correlation show?
How to use PROC CORR
Getting subset correlations
How PROC CORR handles missing values

You can use the SAS procedure CORR to get correlation coefficients.

What does correlation show?

Correlation analysis is used to measure the strength of the relationship between two variables.

When two variables are positively correlated, observations that have high values of one variable also tend to have high values of the other. For example, height and weight are correlated. Although there are exceptions, generally a low height value and a low weight value tend to be found in the same individual.

When two variables are not correlated, there is no apparent linear relationship between the values of one and the values of the other.

When two variables are negatively correlated, high values of one variable tend to be associated with low values of the other variable. For example, bond prices tend to rise when the interest rate falls.

Correlation coefficients range from –1 to 1. A correlation coefficient close to 1 means that the two variables are positively correlated; a correlation coefficient near zero means there is little correlation between the values of the two variables; and a correlation coefficient close to –1 means that the variables are negatively correlated.

How to use PROC CORR

To get correlation coefficients (Pearson product-moment) for all the numeric variables in the most recently created SAS data set, use the PROC CORR statement alone:

PROC CORR;

```
VARIABLE     N      MEAN      STD DEV       SUM     MINIMUM     MAXIMUM

AGE         19  13.3157895  1.4926722    253.00000  11.0000000   16.000000
HEIGHT      19  61.9473684  5.1905222   1177.00000  51.0000000   72.000000
WEIGHT      19  99.8421053 22.8187622   1897.00000  50.0000000  150.000000

PEARSON CORRELATION COEFFICIENTS / PROB > |R| UNDER HO:RHO=0 / N = 19

                       AGE     HEIGHT   WEIGHT

           AGE      1.00000   0.81254   0.74042
                    0.0000    0.0001    0.0003

           HEIGHT   0.81254   1.00000   0.87800
                    0.0001    0.0000    0.0001

           WEIGHT   0.74042   0.87800   1.00000
                    0.0003    0.0001    0.0000
```

figure 10-1

To get correlation coefficients for another data set, use DATA= in the PROC CORR statement:

PROC CORR DATA = LASTYR;

To get correlation coefficients for some, but not all, of the numeric variables in the data set, list the variables you want in a VAR statement:

PROC CORR;
  VAR HEIGHT WEIGHT;

Getting subset correlations

You can get correlation coefficients for subsets of your data with PROC CORR and a BY statement. For example, say you wanted to get correlations first for the females and then for the males. You would use a BY statement with PROC CORR:

PROC CORR;
  BY SEX;

Remember that before you can use a BY statement with a SAS procedure, the data set must already be sorted in the order of the variables in the BY statement. So you may need to use PROC SORT before you get correlations:

PROC SORT;
  BY SEX;
PROC CORR;
  BY SEX;

How PROC CORR handles missing values

When PROC CORR calculates the correlation coefficient for two variables, it leaves out any observation that has a missing value for either of the two variables.

Chapter 11

Analysis of Variance

by Kathryn A. Council

What is analysis of variance?
A typical experiment
Terminology
How to use the SAS System for analysis of variance
Balanced vs. unbalanced data
Experimental designs

What is analysis of variance?

Analysis of variance is a statistical technique that is used to study the variability of experimental data. For example, you might observe that using different fertilizers on tomato plants results in the production of different amounts of tomatoes. This difference in tomato yield is the *variability*. You can use analysis of variance to see if such factors as the fertilizer contribute to that variability.

The basic process that takes place when you use analysis of variance is testing hypotheses about your data—for example, you might hypothesize that the fertilizer does not significantly affect the tomato yield.

The hypotheses are often stated in terms of the equality of group means. For example, you might classify the yields from the tomato plants into three groups, one for each fertilizer you used, and then state your hypothesis as, "The mean tomato yield does not differ significantly among the three fertilizer groups."

A typical experiment

Let's follow the tomato plant experiment through the experimental stage and into the analysis phase.

You buy a dozen tomato plants of the same variety. To reduce the variability from factors other than fertilizer, you choose plants that are as alike as possible and pot them in the same type of soil.

You select four of the plants at random and use fish-oil emulsion as the fertilizer, applying it weekly. Four other plants receive Magic-Grow fertilizer weekly. The last four plants are allowed to grow with just the nutrients in the soil—no fertilizer. During the growing season, you record the weight of the tomatoes produced by each plant, and after the first frost you calculate the total weight for each plant. This total weight is the plant's *yield*.

Now you formulate the hypothesis that the mean yield does not differ significantly among the three fertilizer groups, and you use the SAS procedure ANOVA to test your hypothesis.

Terminology

In the terminology of analysis of variance, the tomato plants in this experiment are *experimental units*. The yield is the *response variable* or the dependent variable. The fertilizer is the *treatment variable*, or independent variable or factor or classification variable.

The variance in plant behavior from treatment to treatment is the *between-group variance*: our hypothesis states that this variance is not significant.

Another kind of variation is also occurring due to the natural variations in the tomato plants, say in their insect infestations. Although you try to reduce this variation by choosing similar plants and potting them in the same soil, it can't be eliminated entirely. This variation is important because it influences the outcome of the experiment, but can't be attributed to the fertilizer treatment. This variance is the *within-group variance*, because it occurs from plant to plant within each treatment group rather than from treatment to treatment. It is also known as the *experimental error*, or the *error*.

How to use the SAS System for analysis of variance

To use SAS for analysis of variance you need a PROC ANOVA statement, a CLASSES statement giving the classification or grouping variables, and a MODEL statement describing the experiment you are investigating. Here are the statements needed for the tomato plant experiment:

PROC ANOVA;
  CLASSES FERTILZR;
  MODEL YIELD = FERTILZR;

The CLASSES statement gives the variable FERTILZR, since we are classifying the experimental units into groups according to which fertilizer treatment they received.

In the MODEL statement, the word MODEL is followed by the variable whose behavior you are studying—the dependent variable or response variable. In this case, you are studying the YIELD. Then comes an equal sign, then the treatment variable, FERTILZR.

The statements

DATA TOMATO;
  INPUT PLANT FERTILZR $ YIELD;
  CARDS;
data lines go here
PROC ANOVA;
  CLASSES FERTILZR;
  MODEL YIELD = FERTILZR;
  TITLE 'TOMATO PLANT EXPERIMENT';

produce the output shown in figure 11-1.

```
                    TOMATO PLANT EXPERIMENT
                 ANALYSIS OF VARIANCE PROCEDURE
                    CLASS LEVEL INFORMATION
                 CLASS      LEVELS     VALUES
                 FERTILZR     3        F M N

            NUMBER OF OBSERVATIONS IN DATA SET = 12


DEPENDENT VARIABLE: YIELD

    SOURCE                 DF      SUM OF SQUARES        MEAN SQUARE      F VALUE

    MODEL                   2       405.50000000       202.75000000       64.03

    ERROR                   9        28.50000000         3.16666667      PR > F

    CORRECTED TOTAL        11       434.00000000                          0.0001


    R-SQUARE             C.V.            ROOT MSE          YIELD MEAN

    0.934332           19.7724          1.77951304         9.00000000


    SOURCE                 DF          ANOVA SS     F VALUE    PR > F

    FERTILZR                2       405.50000000     64.03     0.0001
```

figure 11-1

Balanced vs. unbalanced data

When all the subgroups of your data contain the same number of observations, you can use PROC ANOVA.

If the subgroups contain different numbers of observations, or if some subgroups contain no observations, use PROC GLM. (ANOVA may be used for unbalanced data when you have only one treatment variable.) All MODEL statements discussed in the following sections can be used with both PROC ANOVA and PROC GLM.[1]

Experimental designs

It's possible to specify any experimental design using the MODEL statement in ANOVA or GLM. Some examples of MODEL statements for basic designs are shown below.

Completely randomized design In the completely randomized design, treatments are assigned to experimental units completely at random. Our tomato plant experiment is an example of a completely randomized design. In this case, the treatment variable, fertilizer, defines the groups. The treatment means, the mean yields of tomatoes per plant for each fertilizer treatment, can be tested for equality:

PROC ANOVA;
  CLASSES FERTILZR;
  MODEL YIELD = FERTILZR;

The source of variation shown on the ANOVA output would be

FERTILZR

and you would use the F value to test whether the mean yield of tomatoes was significantly different for the three fertilizer treatments. If this F value was significant, then you would not accept the hypothesis that the means are equal. You would thus conclude that at least one of the fertilizer treatments caused a different tomato yield.

The analysis of variance tells you *if* there are differences; it does not tell you the nature of these differences. It does not tell you which fertilizer treatments produced different results, or in which direction these differences were. The data themselves give clues to this information, but further analyses are often required.

Randomized block design   In the randomized block design, experimental units are first grouped into blocks so that the experimental error within each block is as small as possible. Then the treatments are assigned at random to the units within each block.

Suppose that you have four areas in your back yard that you feel would work equally well as gardens for the tomatoes. You plant three tomato plants in each area and apply the fertilizer treatments at random to the plants in each area. Since the soil in each area is about the same, you don't expect the fertilizer treatments to affect the plants differently in the different areas. In other words, we assume that there is no block*treatment (area*fertilizer) interaction.

The tomato plants should behave similarly, except for fertilizer differences, in the same area, and we can filter out the variation among areas from the experimental error by using a randomized block design with AREA as the blocking factor:

PROC ANOVA;
  CLASSES FERTILZR AREA;
  MODEL YIELD = AREA FERTILZR;

The sources of variation on the ANOVA output would be

FERTILZR
AREA

and the F value shown beside each of these sources would be used to test whether the yield of tomatoes was significantly different for the fertilizers, as before; the additional test would show whether the means were different for the different areas.

If this latter test is significant, it tells us that including the source of variation due to area in our design was a good idea, since without it the variation among areas would have been part of the experimental error. It also tells us that at least one of the areas in the back yard is probably better for tomatoes than the others.

Since we still have the same number of tomato plants, we must still have the same total degrees of freedom. Thus, the degrees of freedom associated with AREA have to come from our previous error degrees of freedom. Often, when deciding the kind of design to use for an experiment, this loss of degrees of freedom in the error term should be considered.

Latin-square design In the Latin-square design, experimental units are grouped twice—into rows and columns—as if you had two blocking factors, so that differences within any row or column are at a minimum. Then the treatments are applied at random so that each treatment occurs in each row and column. When treatment means are compared, the variation due to rows and the variation due to columns are both taken out of the error term.

Suppose, for example, that the tomato plant experiment was set up a little differently. This time we have only three areas in the back yard. In each area we use three different methods for supporting the plants—chicken-wire cages, tomato stakes, and no support. In case these support methods cause differences in the yield, we want to be able to filter the differences out from the experimental error. We assume that no interactions exist in the experiment—that is, no interaction exists between area and fertilizer, support and fertilizer, or support and area.

Fertilizer treatments are then assigned at random to the plants in each area so that each treatment occurs once in each row and each column. One of the permutations of the design would look like this:

| | | SUPPORT | | |
		cages	stakes	no support
	1	fish oil	Magic-Grow	no fertilizer
AREA	2	no fertilizer	fish oil	Magic-Grow
	3	Magic-Grow	no fertilizer	fish oil

This is a 3 x 3 Latin-square design, and these SAS statements are used:

```
PROC ANOVA;
    CLASSES AREA SUPPORT FERTILZR;
    MODEL YIELD = FERTILZR AREA SUPPORT;
```

Sources of variation would be

AREA
SUPPORT
FERTILZR

and the associated F values would test for differences in YIELD for treatments (FERTILZR), for row (AREA), and for columns (SUPPORT).

Factorial experiment In a factorial experiment, the effects of several different factors are considered simultaneously. The *design* of the experiment may be completely randomized, randomized block, or some other design.

Suppose, for example, that in addition to testing the different fertilizers on the tomatoes, we also want to test the effect of watering each plant once a week with one gallon against the effect of watering each plant three times a week, one gallon at a time.

This, then, is a 3 x 2 factorial. The first factor, FERTILZR, has three levels (fish oil, Magic-Grow, and none) and the second factor, WATER, has two levels (1 gallon weekly and 3 gallons weekly). A treatment consists of a certain combination of these two factors: for example, no fertilizer with 1 gallon of water per week, or fish oil with 3 gallons per week. In fact, the total number of treatments would be the number of possible combinations of each factor's levels—in this case, six.

Not only do you want to determine if there are differences in the weight of the tomatoes depending on the fertilizer treatments, and between the watering methods, but you also want to determine if an interaction exists between the FERTILZR and WATER factors. Fertilizer may have more of an effect on the plants that are watered three times a week than on those watered only once a week.

For simplicity, let's assume that all twelve of the plants are back in pots, all are supported by tomato cages, and all are in the same area of the yard. If two plants are chosen at random to receive the first treatment, two more are chosen at random to receive the second treatment and so on, then this is a completely randomized design with factorial treatments:

PROC ANOVA;
  CLASSES FERTILZR WATER;
  MODEL YIELD = FERTILZR WATER FERTILZR*WATER;

Sources of variation would be

FERTILZR
WATER
FERTILZR*WATER

(If only one plant had been assigned to each treatment, all the degrees of freedom would have been used in the FERTILZR, WATER, and FERTILZR* WATER sources, so that no error term would have been present. To avoid this situation, this example uses two plants for each treatment.)

If you test for the presence of a significant FERTILZR*WATER effect and find that this interaction is not significant, testing for significant FERTILZR and WATER main effects is appropriate. If the interaction is significant, care should be exercised in interpreting the main effects of FERTILZR and WATER.

Nested classifications In a design with nested classifications, an extra factor is introduced that is "nested" within another factor. For example, leaves of a plant would be nested within the plant; cows would be nested within a herd.

In this situation, you would not consider the cross-classification of leaves with plants, since leaf 1 from plant 1 is different from leaf 1 from any other plant.

Nested classifications are specified in a MODEL statement as

PROC ANOVA;
  CLASSES PLANT LEAF;
  MODEL RESPONSE = PLANT LEAF(PLANT);

---

[1] When SAS performs an analysis of variance, the mean square of the error term is used for computing F values. For some designs, other tests are required: for example, in a split-plot design. In these cases, a TEST statement should be used to specify which terms in the model are to be used as both numerator and denominator in the F test.

Regression[1]

by John P. Sall

Linear regression is a statistical procedure used when you want to study relationships between variables. For example, you might hypothesize that population increases as time passes. You want to see if the relationship between population and time can be described by this equation:

population = coefficient*time + constant

You use regression to estimate the values of the coefficient and the constant.

Regression has many uses:

- learning if one variable can be expressed in terms of another
- predicting one variable's values from another's values.

Regression terminology

The equation of a straight line is

$y = ax + b$

If you take two x values,
multiply each x value by a,
add b to each product of a and x to get two y values,
then plot the y values against the x values,

you get a straight line. This straight line intercepts the y axis at b, so b is called the *intercept*. The *coefficient, a,* is the slope of the straight line: it represents the change in y for each unit change in x.

Say you have a set of *y* values—call them the Y variable—and a set of *x* values, the X variable. You believe that Y depends on X, and you formulate a *model* of Y's behavior as it relates to X:

Y = coefficient*X + intercept

When you plot Y against X, you get a scatter diagram:

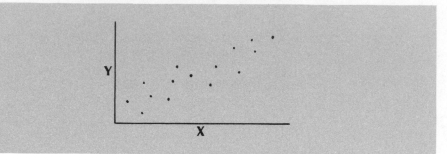

figure 12-1

For an estimate of the equation of the straight line that best fits the points on this scatter diagram, you use regression. You know the X and Y values for this equation; regression gives you the coefficient—the slope of the line—and the intercept. Plotting the *regression equation*

Y = coefficient*X + intercept

gives you the *regression line*—the line that best fits the points on the graph.

Since we are studying Y's dependence on X, Y is known as the *dependent variable* or *response variable*. X is the *independent variable*, or *regressor*, or *factor*.

Studying Y's dependence on more than one variable is *multiple regression*. In multiple regression, you are estimating a coefficient for each independent variable. For example, this is a regression equation for two independent variables:

Y = coefficient$_1$*X1 + coefficient$_2$*X2 + intercept

The principle of least squares

How do we know what the best-fitting straight line is?

Say we draw a straight line through the cluster of points on the scatter diagram. Then, for each point, we find its vertical distance from the straight line, square this distance, and then add together all the squared distances. Of all the lines that could possibly be drawn on the graph, *the best-fitting line is the one with the smallest sum of squared distances*.

The distance from a point to the straight line is a *residual*—the difference between the actual Y value and the Y value that the regression equation predicts. The residuals represent the behavior of Y that the independent variables don't account for—the error in the model.

If we assume that the model is correct—that no independent variables have been left out that should have been included, that a straight line does describe the relationship between the variables; and if we also make the assumption that the true residuals are normally and independently distributed, with a mean of zero and constant variance, we can test hypotheses, assign confidence regions, and compute significance probabilities.

GLM stands for **G**eneral **L**inear **M**odel, and GLM estimates and tests hypotheses about linear models. To use GLM, you need a PROC GLM statement and a MODEL statement defining the model whose coefficients you want to estimate.

Simple regression

Continuing with the population example, say you want to study the dependence of population on time. In your SAS data set, you have a variable POP containing U.S. population levels and a variable YEAR containing the years corresponding to the populations. POP is the dependent variable, YEAR the independent variable.

These statements ask for a regression of POP on YEAR:

PROC GLM;
  MODEL POP = YEAR;

In the MODEL statement, the dependent variable appears first, then an equal sign (=), then the independent variable.

GLM's output

GLM always estimates a constant term (the intercept) unless otherwise directed, and a coefficient for each independent variable.

The GLM printout (see figure 12-2) is organized into four sections:

- overall analysis of variance table
- miscellaneous statistics
- results for special TYPE I and TYPE III tests
- report on the parameter estimates.

GENERAL LINEAR MODELS PROCEDURE

DEPENDENT VARIABLE: POP

SOURCE	DF	SUM OF SQUARES	MEAN SQUARE	F VALUE
MODEL	1	66336.46922569	66336.46922569	201.87
ERROR	17	5586.29252905	328.60544289	PR > F
CORRECTED TOTAL	18	71922.76175474		0.0001

R-SQUARE	C.V.	ROOT MSE	POP MEAN
0.922329	25.9827	18.12747757	69.76747368

SOURCE	DF	TYPE I SS	F VALUE	PR > F
YEAR	1	66336.46922569	201.87	0.0001

SOURCE	DF	TYPE III SS	F VALUE	PR > F
YEAR	1	66336.46922569	201.87	0.0001

PARAMETER	ESTIMATE	T FOR H0: PARAMETER=0	PR > |T|	STD ERROR OF ESTIMATE
INTERCEPT	-1958.36630175	-13.71	0.0001	142.80454644
YEAR	1.07879456	14.21	0.0001	0.07592765

figure 12-2

Analysis of variance table   The overall analysis of variance table breaks down the total sum of squares for the dependent variable into the portion attributed to our model and the portion that the model does not account for, which is attributed to error.

The mean square term is the sum of squares divided by the degrees of freedom (DF). The mean square for error (MS(ERROR)) is an estimate of σ^2, the variance of the true residuals.

Miscellaneous statistics:

MODEL F   This value (in figure 12-2, 201.87) is the ratio produced by dividing MS(MODEL) by MS(ERROR). It tests how well the model as a whole (after adjusting for the mean) accounts for the dependent variable's behavior. If the significance probability, labeled PR>F, is small, it indicates significance.

R-SQUARE R^2 measures how much variation in the dependent variable can be accounted for by the model. R^2, which can range from 0 to 1, is the ratio of the sum of squares for the model divided by the sum of squares for the corrected total. Our value in figure 12-2 of .922329 indicates that we can account for over 92% of the population just by knowing the year. In general, the larger the value of R^2, the better the model's fit.

C.V.   This measure is the coefficient of variation and is often used to describe the amount of variation in the population. It is equal to the standard deviation of the dependent variable (ROOT MSE) divided by the mean of the dependent variable, times 100. The coefficient of variation is often a preferred measure because it is unitless.

ROOT MSE   This is the square root of MS(ERROR) and is also known as the standard deviation of the dependent variable.

dep MEAN   This is the mean of the dependent variable. In this case, it is the overall mean of the variable POP.

Results for special TYPE I and TYPE III tests   These tests are used primarily in analysis of variance applications. The TYPE I SS measures incremental sums of squares for the model as each variable is added. The TYPE III SS is the sum of squares due to adding that variable last in the model. In our example, since only one independent variable was included in the model, both these sums of squares are equal to each other and also to the sum of squares for the model shown in the overall analysis of variance table.

The F VALUE and PR>F values for TYPE III tests in this section of the output are equivalent to the results of a *t* test for testing the hypothesis that the regression parameter equals zero.

Report on the parameter estimates   This section of the output gives the estimates for the model parameters—the intercept and the coefficients. In figure 12-2, the INTERCEPT estimate is –1958.36630175, and the estimate of YEAR's coefficient is 1.07879456. "T FOR H0: PARAMETER = 0" means "the *t* value for testing the null hypothesis that the parameter equals zero." In figure 12-2, the *t* value for testing the hypothesis that the intercept equals zero is –13.71.

The value given in the table for PR>|T| answers the question, "If the parameter is really equal to zero, what is the probability of getting a larger value of *t*?" Thus, a very small value for this probability indicates that the value of the parameter is not likely to equal zero, and therefore that the independent variable contributes significantly to the model. In figure 12-2, both PR>|T| values are .0001. Thus, you would not accept the hypothesis that the intercept is equal to zero, nor the hypothesis that the YEAR coefficient equals zero. You conclude that the independent variable YEAR does contribute significantly to the model.

Exploring the population example

You want to describe the historical growth of the United States population using regression techniques. You know that many factors influence population growth, but you want to see how population increases can be described purely in terms of the passage of time.

Your data You get the data from census statistics reported in an almanac. To keep the numbers more manageable, you represent the population in millions. One use of regression is prediction, and you decide to use the model for prediction. Consequently, your last three observations have only values for YEAR—no POP values. You will use the model to predict these missing population values.

You can get a good picture of the relationship between population and year by plotting the data, since there are only two variables in the model.

```
DATA POP;
  INPUT POP YEAR;
  CARDS;
data lines go here
PROC PLOT;
  PLOT POP*YEAR;
```

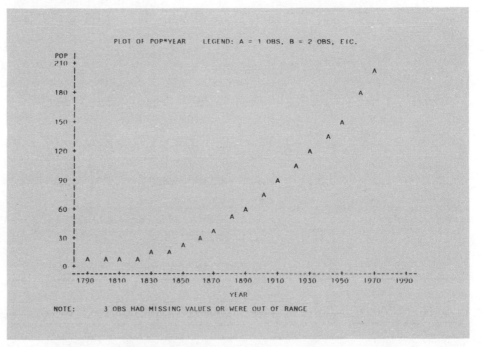

figure 12-3

It is easy to see the positive growth trend in figure 12-3, since as the years increase, so does population.

To find the regression line for these data, you use the SAS statements

PROC GLM;
  MODEL POP = YEAR;

The resulting printout, described above, is shown in figure 12-2.

Everything in the printout indicates that you have achieved a good fit with the model. However, you want to examine the model further, and you begin with the residuals.

Getting residuals and predicted values To get residuals and predicted values in a new SAS data set, use an OUTPUT statement with the PROC GLM and MODEL statements:

PROC GLM;
  MODEL POP = YEAR;
  OUTPUT OUT = NEW P = PREDICT R = RESID;

The OUTPUT statement asks GLM to create a new SAS data set. The name appearing after OUT= in the OUTPUT statement gives the name you want the new data set to have. In this case, you choose the name NEW.

The name appearing after P= in the OUTPUT statement gives the name you want the variable containing the predicted values to have in the new data set. For each observation in the data set, GLM inserts the YEAR value into the regression equation and finds a predicted population value. These predicted population values become the PREDICT variable in the data set NEW.

The name appearing after R= in the OUTPUT statement gives the name that you want the variable containing the residuals to have in the new data set. For each observation in the original data set, GLM subtracts the population value predicted by the model from the actual POP value in that observation: the difference between the two values is the residual, and the residual values become the variable RESID in data set NEW.

If the dependent variable's value is missing for an observation, as the POP value is for the last three observations in this example, the RESID value will also be missing for those observations. The PREDICT variable will contain the projected population values for those years, as predicted by the model.

Analyzing residuals and predicted values Using the data set NEW containing the residuals and the predicted values, we can plot the predicted population values against the actual POP values and the residuals against the actual values:

PROC PLOT;
  PLOT POP*YEAR PREDICT*YEAR = 'P' / OVERLAY;
  PLOT RESID*YEAR / VREF = 0;

The first PLOT statement asks for a plot of the original POP values against the YEAR values and then for a plot of the PREDICTed population values against YEAR, with the letter P used for the points in the second plot. The OVERLAY option after the slash (/) asks that these two plots appear on the same page.

The second PLOT statement asks for a plot of the residuals against the YEAR value, and the VREF = 0 option after the slash (/) draws a line on the graph at zero on the vertical axis.

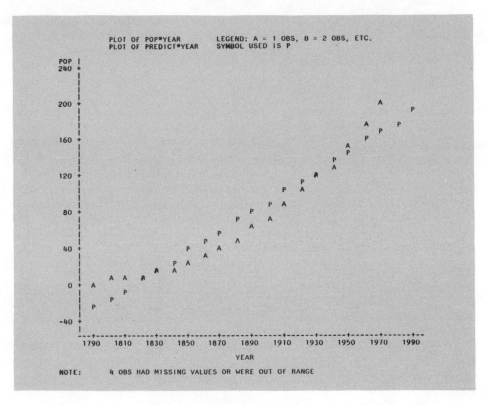

figure 12-4

In figure 12-4, the Ps represent the regression line. Several problems are obvious:

- the model predicts negative population values for the years up to 1810!
- although the actual values, denoted by As, and the predicted values, denoted by Ps, are very close to each other on the graph, close examination shows that for the years between 1840 and 1910, all the actual values fall *below* the regression line. For a good fit, actual values should be equally scattered.

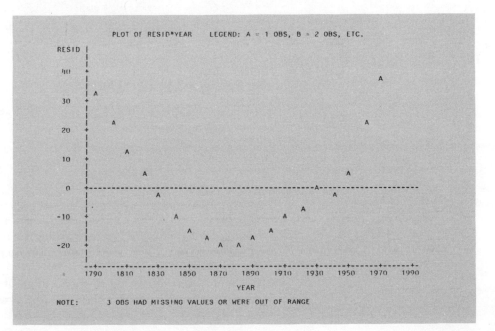

figure 12-5

The plot of residuals, in figure 12-5, shows dramatically that our model is not such a good one. Residuals should be scattered randomly about the line drawn on the graph, which represents zero.

In this case, the residuals seem to move in a pattern, which suggests that another model is appropriate—perhaps a quadratic or polynomial equation.

Multiple regression The goal of regression analysis is to account for the changes in the dependent variable. If a single independent variable fails to account for most of the change, it is natural to hypothesize that the dependent variable depends on two or more independent variables. For example, we might hypothesize that population (POP) depends on both time (YEAR) and the annual immigration into the U.S. (IMMIGRAT):

PROC GLM;
   MODEL POP = YEAR IMMIGRAT;

Since both YEAR and IMMIGRAT are independent variables, they appear on the right-hand side of the MODEL statement.

Polynomial regression You can treat polynomial regression—where you have a term in the model whose values have been squared or otherwise powered—as a multiple regression.

First you create a new variable YEARSQ by squaring the YEAR values. You then include YEARSQ in the MODEL statement along with YEAR:

DATA POP;
   INPUT POP YEAR;
   YEARSQ = YEAR*YEAR;
   CARDS;
data lines
PROC GLM;
   MODEL POP = YEAR YEARSQ;

Or you can include the polynomial term YEAR*YEAR in the MODEL statement when you are using GLM:

PROC GLM;
   MODEL POP = YEAR YEAR*YEAR;

(This special feature for indicating polynomial terms is not available in the other SAS regression procedures.)

When we examine the output from this GLM run (figure 12-6), we notice:

- R-SQUARE has increased from .922 to .998, the F value from 201 to 4641—the model does fit the data better.
- The TYPE I SS for YEAR is the same as it was before for the one-variable model, because the TYPE I SS measures the first-to-enter. The TYPE I SS for YEAR*YEAR, the last term into the model, is the same as the TYPE III SS for YEAR*YEAR.
- The parameters all test significantly different from zero. If the population growth was really linear, rather than quadratic, we probably would have seen the YEAR*YEAR term test as not significant.

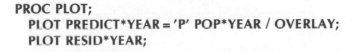

figure 12-6

We plot the residuals as we did before:

```
PROC PLOT;
    PLOT PREDICT*YEAR = 'P' POP*YEAR / OVERLAY;
    PLOT RESID*YEAR;
```

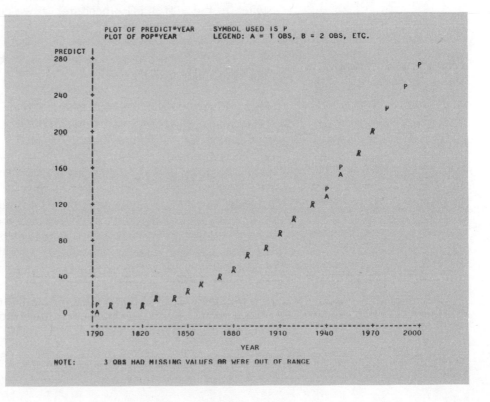

figure 12-7

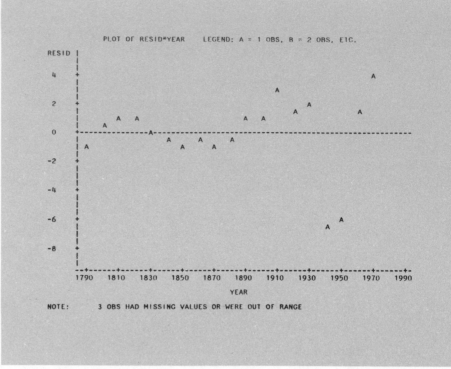

figure 12-7 continued

The actual values track the line of fit very closely this time. The residuals look much better, but there still is some pattern. This pattern might be the result of autocorrelation—we could use the P option in GLM to get a Durbin-Watson statistic to check for this. If we found autocorrelation to be a problem, we could switch to the AUTOREG procedure. Or we could try higher-order polynomial models—but don't rely on this method too heavily. Polynomials above five or so terms are notorious for producing ill-conditioning in the arithmetic, and the line of fit might dance around in strange ways between the data values. Other functions might be suggested.

Another problem with the residuals plotted in figure 12-7 concerns the 1940 and 1950 values, which are suspiciously far out. If we know a little U.S. history, this is to be expected, since the years 1930-1950 had very low birth rates due to a severe economic depression followed by a major war. These values should thus probably be treated as special cases. How can we do this?

Dummy variables Let's assume that 1940 and 1950 are special cases of a very temporary nature—that the baby boom after the war made up for the temporary effect, and that the rest of the values are back on the path. Then we can create a "dummy variable" that has the value of 1 for those two observations, and 0 for the rest.

The parameter for the dummy variable will then measure the difference of the population for these two observations from the overall fit. The *t* statistic will test whether they differ from the quadratic trend.

We create a new data set with the dummy variable, then run GLM with DUMMY as the third term in the model:

```
DATA POP2;
  SET POP;
  IF YEAR = 1940 OR YEAR = 1950 THEN DUMMY = 1;
  ELSE DUMMY = 0;
PROC GLM DATA = POP2;
  MODEL POP = YEAR YEAR*YEAR DUMMY;
  OUTPUT OUT = P3 R = RESID;
```

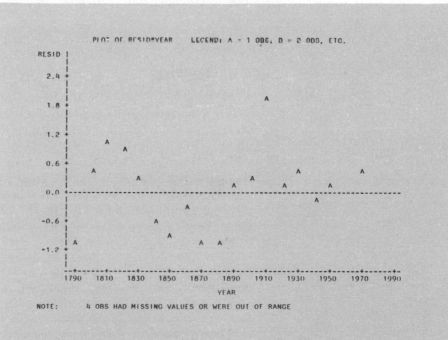

figure 12-8

figure 12-9

The output of the model using the dummy variable appears in figure 12-8. R-SQUARE has jumped to .9998. The DUMMY variable is highly significant, and the deviation of 1940-1950 from the trend is estimated to be –8.7 million in population. The estimates for the other parameters in the model did not change much, although the standard errors improved a lot. The plot of the residuals, shown in figure 12-9, is the same as before except that the two former outliers are no longer far out; this changed the scale of the plot.

Although additional exploratory analysis should continue on this set of data—for example, nonlinear regression analysis—we will stop at this point.

It is always important to investigate your data thoroughly in any analysis. In this example, although it looked initially as though we had achieved a good fit, we discovered certain problems with the model after studying it more thoroughly. One of the purposes of this example was to show what can happen to the unwary user unless he takes certain precautions and studies his data carefully.

Other regression procedures

Stepwise regression In some situations, you may have many variables that might contribute to the behavior of a dependent variable. In this case, you have two goals:

- to provide an equation that is useful for prediction—one that has an R^2 close to 1
- to provide an equation that is economical—one that uses only a few independent variables.

These goals seem to contradict one another since, in general, an equation involving three variables will have a higher R^2 than any equation involving only two of the variables.

This is a situation in which the STEPWISE procedure is appropriate. STEPWISE performs stepwise regression, which is an attempt to search for the "best" model by bringing into the regression equation the independent variables one by one.

In this case, the statements

PROC STEPWISE;
   MODEL Y = X1 X2 X3 X4;

perform a regression analysis on the "best" one-variable model, then the "best" two-variable model, and so on. The output from STEPWISE is similar to the GLM output.

All possible regressions When you are searching for a model, another solution is the RSQUARE procedure in SAS. This procedure gives the variables included in the model, along with the associated R^2, for all possible combinations of the independent variables in the MODEL statement.

RSQUARE is often appropriate when you have a large number of independent variables that you want to try for the initial stages of an analysis. Once you have examined all possible models, you can select several likely ones and use GLM with them.

---

[1] This chapter provides a bare introduction to regression. If you are unfamiliar with regression, study a good statistics text to learn more about implied assumptions, statistical terminology, properties of estimators and hypothesis tests, and problems in using regression.

Chapter 13

Writing Custom-Tailored Reports

In Chapter 6 we discussed PROC PRINT to print reports. PROC PRINT is useful for printing lists of variable values, but you will probably want to also print reports that are tailored to specific needs. You can use the PUT statement to print these reports.

The PUT statement The PUT statement asks the SAS System to print information. PUT statements are SAS program statements: they appear in the DATA step and they are carried out for *each* observation that the DATA step processes.

The INPUT statement, which we discussed in Chapter 2, reads data lines; the PUT statement prints data lines. Although these two statements produce opposite effects, most of the same rules apply to both INPUT and PUT statements.

For example, the INPUT statement to read the height-weight data lines was

INPUT NAME $ 1–10 SEX $ 12 AGE 14–15 HEIGHT 17–18 WEIGHT 20–22;

The PUT statement that would print the data in exactly the form they have on the input lines is

PUT NAME 1–10 SEX 12 AGE 14–15 HEIGHT 17–18 WEIGHT 20–22;

The information that you can ask SAS to print with a PUT statement falls into two categories:

- variable values
- constant values.

Variable values

To print the values of a variable, give the variable name in the PUT statement. For example, the PUT statement in the job below asks SAS to print the values of the variable NAME:

DATA NEW1;
   INPUT NAME $ 1–10 SEX $ 12 AGE HEIGHT WEIGHT;
   PUT NAME;
   CARDS;
BERNADETTE   F   13 65 84
JEFFREY   M   13 62 84
MARY   F   15 66 112

```
BERNADETTE
JEFFREY
MARY
```

figure 13-1

SAS carries out the PUT statement once for each observation, printing the value of NAME for that observation.

Named output

You can print the name of the variable before the value of the variable by putting an equal sign after the variable name in the PUT statement:

PUT NAME = ;

Then SAS labels the values with the variable name. Here is an example:

DATA NEW2;
   INPUT NAME $ 1–10;
   PUT NAME = ;
   CARDS;
BERNADETTE
JEFFREY
MARY

```
NAME=BERNADETTE
NAME=JEFFREY
NAME=MARY
```

figure 13-2

Constant values

To print the same information each time the PUT statement is carried out, give the information you want printed as a constant in the PUT statement.

A *constant* consists of from 1 to 200 characters enclosed in single quotes. For example, the PUT statement below asks SAS to print the constant 'NAME OF STUDENT IS' each time that the PUT statement is carried out:

DATA NEW3;
   INPUT NAME $ 1–10;
   PUT 'NAME OF STUDENT IS';
   CARDS;
BERNADETTE
JEFFREY
MARY

```
NAME OF STUDENT IS
NAME OF STUDENT IS
NAME OF STUDENT IS
```

figure 13-3

Combining variables and constants in PUT statements

You can combine variables and constants in the PUT statement. For example, the PUT statement below asks SAS to print for every observation first the constant 'NAME OF STUDENT IS' and then the value of the variable NAME:

```
DATA NEW4;
   INPUT NAME $ 1–10;
   PUT 'NAME OF STUDENT IS ' NAME;
   CARDS;
BERNADETTE
JEFFREY
MARY
```

```
NAME OF STUDENT IS BERNADETTE
NAME OF STUDENT IS JEFFREY
NAME OF STUDENT IS MARY
```

figure 13-4

Positioning variables and constants in specific columns

When SAS carries out a PUT statement, it ordinarily begins to print in the first column of a new line.

You can position values in specific columns on the output lines by giving the column numbers after the variable name or constant in the PUT statement. For example, the statement

PUT NAME 1–10;

prints each NAME value in columns 1-10 of a new line.

You need not put a dollar sign after character variables in the PUT statement, as you do in INPUT statements, because SAS knows they are character variables.

To print variables with decimal parts, give the number of decimal places after the columns. For example, this statement prints values of the numeric variable YIELD with one decimal place:

PUT YIELD 14–17 .1;

Remember to allow enough columns to print the decimal point.

The @ symbol You can also use the symbol @ *before* the variable name or constant in the PUT statement to position printing. The column number where you want printing to begin accompanies the @. For example, the statement

PUT @15 NAME;

asks SAS to go to column 15 of a new line, then to print the NAME value.

You may use as many @ symbols in PUT statements as you need. For example, the statement

PUT @15 NAME @28 'IS THE STUDENT NAME';

asks SAS to move to column 15 of a new line, then to print the NAME value, then to skip to column 28 and print the constant 'IS THE STUDENT NAME'.

It's possible to use the @ symbol with numeric variables. But until you are ready to use SAS formats to print numeric values, you should stick with giving the columns you want the numeric values printed in, plus the number of decimal places you want:

PUT X 27–30 .2;

SAS formats A *format* is shorthand to SAS to print a value in a special form. For example, the SAS format DOLLAR. following a variable name in a PUT statement tells SAS to print the variable's values preceded by a dollar sign, with commas between every three digits. For example, using the statement

PUT AMT DOLLAR.;

to print the value 2366 produces

$2,366

Skipping lines

You can ask SAS to print more than one line each time it carries out a PUT statement by using the symbol / when you want to skip to the next line. For example, the SAS statement

PUT @15 NAME / HEIGHT 18–19;

asks SAS to begin printing each NAME value in column 15 of a new line, then to skip to the next line, and to print the corresponding HEIGHT value in columns 18 and 19 of that line.

Where to write output lines: the FILE statement

The output lines that PUT statements produce ordinarily are printed on the SAS log at the end of the DATA step statements.

You can use the FILE statement to tell SAS where to write output lines. For example, the statement FILE PRINT asks SAS to print the output lines produced by the PUT statement in the same place as procedure output:

```
DATA ONE;
    INPUT NAME $ 1–10 SEX $ 12;
    FILE PRINT;
    PUT 'THE NAME OF THE STUDENT IS ' NAME;
    CARDS;
data lines
```

To punch the output lines, use the FILE PUNCH statement:

```
DATA TWO;
    INPUT NAME $ 1–10 HEIGHT 17–18 WEIGHT 20–22;
    RATIO = WEIGHT/HEIGHT;
    FILE PUNCH;
    PUT NAME 1–10 RATIO 11–20 .3;
    CARDS;
data lines
```

Getting totals

You can ask SAS to accumulate totals by using a sum statement in the DATA step.

The sum statement consists of a variable name, a plus sign (+), and a number or variable. For example,

N + 1;

is a sum statement. Every time SAS carries out this statement, it adds 1 to the value of N. The N value is saved until the end of the DATA step or until an assignment statement changes the value.

The SAS job below adds YIELD's value to the value of TOTAL each time an observation is processed, and the PUT statement prints the value of TOTAL each time an observation is processed:

```
DATA ADD;
  INPUT ID $ YIELD;
  TOTAL + YIELD;
  PUT TOTAL = ;
  CARDS;
A312    7
B004    14
A691    5
A058    11
B892    8
B105    10
;
```

```
TOTAL=7
TOTAL=21
TOTAL=26
TOTAL=37
TOTAL=45
TOTAL=55
```

figure 13-5

Checking for the last observation

When you use the sum statement to accumulate a total during a DATA step, you usually want to print that total after the sum statement has been carried out for the last observation.

You can check to see whether the current observation is the last one in the data set by using the END= option in the SET statement to define a variable.

Here is an example:

```
DATA TOTAL;
  SET HTWT END = FINAL;
  TOT + 1;
  IF FINAL THEN PUT 'TOTAL STUDENTS IN DATA SET = ' TOT;
```

figure 13-6

```
TOTAL STUDENTS IN THE DATA SET = 19
```

When SAS begins to process the last observation in data set HTWT, it assigns 1 to the value of the variable FINAL for that observation. Before then, FINAL's value is 0. (Because FINAL is a special variable defined with the END= option, SAS does not add it to the data set being created. However, it can be used in program statements.)

The next statement in the example is TOT + 1, the sum statement. SAS adds 1 to the value of TOT each time this statement is carried out.

Next, the IF statement checks the value of FINAL each time SAS processes an observation. Saying "IF FINAL THEN..." is equivalent to "IF FINAL = 1 THEN..." and is simpler.[1]

The BY statement in the DATA step

In Chapter 4 we discussed using the BY statement with PROC steps. You can also use a BY statement with a DATA step under these conditions:

- you are using a SET statement (or MERGE or UPDATE) so that the input data are coming from a SAS data set that you created earlier in the job or in another job
- this data set is sorted by the BY variable.

When you use a BY statement in the DATA step, SAS keeps track of whether the current observation happens to be either the first or the last observation to have a given value of the BY variable.

For example, consider these data:

figure 13-7

```
OBS       NAME          SEX
 1        BERNADETTE     F
 2        SUSAN          F
 3        CAROL          F
 4        HENRY          M
 5        JAMES          M
```

Observation 1 is the first in the data set to have the value 'F' for the variable SEX; observation 4 is the first to have the value 'M' for the variable SEX. Observation 3 is the last to have the value 'F', and observation 5 is the last to have the value 'M' for SEX.

When the current observation is the first in the data set to have a given value of the BY variable, SAS assigns the value 1 to a special variable. The name of this special variable has two parts—the word FIRST, then a period, and then the name of the BY variable.

For example, if your BY statement was

BY SEX;

the special variable's name would be FIRST.SEX.

Likewise, when the current observation is the last in the data set to have a given value of the BY variable SEX, SAS assigns the value 1 to the special variable LAST.SEX.

When the current observation is not the first to have a given value of the BY variable, the value of the FIRST. byvariable is 0. Likewise, when the observation is not the last to have the current value of the BY variable, the value of the LAST. variable is 0.

Below is a SAS job that prints the contents of a data set, then prints the values of the FIRST. and LAST. byvariables. (Although FIRST. and LAST. byvariables are not added to the data set being created, they can be used in program statements just as other variables are used.)

DATA FRSTLAST;
  SET HTWT;
  BY SEX;
  PUT NAME @13 SEX @16 FIRST.SEX= @29 LAST.SEX=;

```
BERNADETTE   F   FIRST.SEX=1   LAST.SEX=0
SUSAN        F   FIRST.SEX=0   LAST.SEX=0
CAROL        F   FIRST.SEX=0   LAST.SEX=1
HENRY        M   FIRST.SEX=1   LAST.SEX=0
JAMES        M   FIRST.SEX=0   LAST.SEX=1
```

figure 13-8

Since BERNADETTE's observation is the first to have a SEX value of 'F', the value of FIRST.SEX is 1. LAST.SEX is 0 for this observation because it is not the last observation with a SEX value of 'F'.

CAROL's observation is the last to have a SEX value of 'F', and LAST.SEX is 1 for this observation.

The next observation is HENRY's, and since it is the first observation to have a SEX value of 'M', FIRST.SEX is again 1. Finally, JAMES' observation is the last observation in the data set to have a SEX value of 'M', and LAST.SEX is again 1.

Saving computer time with __NULL__

In Chapter 2 we said that the DATA statement begins creation of a new SAS set.

When you are using a DATA step for the sole purpose of printing a report, and do not need to create another SAS data set, you can use the special data set name __NULL__ in the DATA statement:

DATA __NULL__;

When __NULL__ is given as the data set name in the DATA statement, SAS carries out the DATA step just as if it were creating a data set, but doesn't put any observations into a data set. Since the computer does less work, you save computer time.

Printing a line only once

You can ask SAS to print a line only once by using the special variable __N__. The value of this variable is 1 the first time SAS executes the DATA step, 2 the second time, and so on. (Although __N__ is not added to the data set being created, it can be used in program statements just as other variables are used.) For example:

IF __N__ = 1 THEN PUT 'DEPT';

causes SAS to print the word DEPT the first time that the DATA step is executed. The statement

IF __N__ = 1 THEN PUT
  '- -';

causes SAS to print a line of hyphens (-).

Printing subtotals

You can use LAST. byvariables and sum statements to print subtotals. For example, the job below prints the total number of observations that have a SEX value of 'F', then prints the same information for observations with a SEX value of 'M':

```
DATA __NULL__;
  SET HTWT;
  BY SEX;
  TOT + 1;
  IF LAST.SEX;
  PUT 'TOTAL FOR ' SEX = 'IS ' TOT;
  TOT = 0;
```

The subsetting IF statement causes SAS to return for another observation immediately unless the value of LAST.SEX is 1, or true. The PUT statement prints the subtotal line when the observation is the last one that has the current value of SEX, whether 'F' or 'M'.

The assignment statement sets the value of TOT to zero once the subtotal has been printed. Then the count starts again for the observations with the next value of SEX.

Printing a report

Your observations are weekly salaries for employees in several departments. You want to get each department's total salaries for the week, and also the total salaries for all departments combined.

First you get the data into a SAS data set:

DATA WEEKLY;
  INPUT NAME $ EMPL__NO DEPT SALARY;
  CARDS;
data lines

Next you sort the data by DEPT and NAME, so that within each department, the observations are alphabetical by name:

DATA WEEKLY;
  INPUT NAME $ EMPL__NO DEPT SALARY;
  CARDS;
data lines
PROC SORT;
  BY DEPT NAME;

Now you are ready to begin the report.

Designing the report

You make a sample of how you want the report to look, and decide in what columns the information should be printed:

```
                      DEPARTMENT SALARIES

   DEPT     EMPLOYEE NUMBER           NAME          SALARY

   XXX           XXXX              XXXXXXXX         XXX.XX
    :             :                   :               :
    :             :                   :               :
  *** DEPARTMENT XXX TOTALS       EMPLOYEES=X      SALARY = $X,XXX.XX
    :             :                   :               :
    :             :                   :               :
  *** DEPARTMENT XXX TOTALS       EMPLOYEES=X      SALARY = $X,XXX.XX

  *** GRAND TOTALS                EMPLOYEES=XX     SALARY= $XX,XXX.XX
```

```
                          DEPARTMENT SALARIES

        DEPT        EMPLOYEE NUMBER          NAME             SALARY
        -----------------------------------------------------------------------
        811             9764                BISHOP           303.90
        811             3571                CANNON           342.40
        811             1211                HALL             544.40
        811             1445                REED             202.00
        811             1710                STRONG           343.20
        811             2267                TUCKER           474.60
        811             1357                WHITE            383.93

     ***DEPARTMENT 811 TOTALS        EMPLOYEES=7           SALARY= $2,594.43

        815             1602                HAMILTON         444.80
        815             1473                HARMER           769.20
        815             1895                LAWRENCE         279.36
        815             2200                MORSE            805.65
        815             1931                RANDOLPH         592.26
        815             2765                ROBERTS          235.85
        815             2688                THOMAS           246.26

     ***DEPARTMENT 815 TOTALS        EMPLOYEES=7           SALARY= $3,373.38

        821             1743                DELL             225.45
        821             1376                FIELDS           469.90
        821             1577                GORLESKI         320.80
        821             1549                HENRY            429.30
        821             1961                NELSON           399.25
        821             4225                SMITH            255.50

     ***DEPARTMENT 821 TOTALS        EMPLOYEES=6           SALARY= $2,100.20

        835             1370                CHARLES          664.60
        835             3416                CONWAY           313.80
        835             1467                LAFFITTE         496.68

     ***DEPARTMENT 835 TOTALS        EMPLOYEES=3           SALARY= $1,475.08

        840             1949                FRANK            708.80
        840             3936                KOSZALKA         334.43
        840             4132                ROGERS           835.00
        840             4234                THORNTON         486.40

     ***DEPARTMENT 840 TOTALS        EMPLOYEES=4           SALARY= $2,364.63


     ***GRAND TOTALS                 EMPLOYEES=27          SALARY=$11,907.72
```

figure 13-9

The SAS statements to print the report

Since what we want here is the report, and not another SAS data set, we can begin with a DATA __NULL__ statement:

DATA WEEKLY;
  INPUT NAME $ EMPL__NO DEPT SALARY;
  CARDS;
data lines
PROC SORT;
  BY DEPT NAME;
DATA __NULL__;

Next comes the SET statement with the END= option:

SET WEEKLY END = FINAL;

Then the BY statement:

BY DEPT;

To print the report on the pages after the SAS log, use a FILE PRINT statement:

FILE PRINT;

Use TITLE and PUT statements to print the lines at the top of the report:

TITLE 'DEPARTMENT SALARIES';
IF __N__ = 1 THEN PUT / @6 'DEPT' @18 'EMPLOYEE NUMBER'
  @43 'NAME' @61 'SALARY';
IF __N__ = 1 THEN PUT
  '- -';

To get departmental totals and the grand total for salaries, add the SALARY value to SUBSAL and TOTSAL; to get departmental totals and the grand total for employees, add 1 to SUBEMP and TOTEMP:

SUBSAL + SALARY;
TOTSAL + SALARY;
SUBEMP + 1;
TOTEMP + 1;

Now, to print each employee's data, write a PUT statement that will be carried out for each observation in the data set:

PUT DEPT 6-8 EMPL__NO 24-27 @ 43 NAME SALARY 59-66 .2;

Unless the current observation is the last one for a given department, we have finished processing the observation. Use a subsetting IF statement to continue processing only for the last observation in a given department:

IF LAST.DEPT;

The remaining statements are carried out only for the last observation in each department.

This PUT statement prints the department totals:

PUT / '*DEPARTMENT ' DEPT 'TOTALS' @31 'EMPLOYEES = '**
  SUBEMP @55 'SALARY = ' SUBSAL DOLLAR10.2 / ;

The SAS format DOLLAR10.2 following SUBSAL tells SAS to use the DOLLAR. format to print the SUBSAL value, with a maximum width of 10 columns and 2 decimal places. The DOLLAR. format prints a dollar sign in front of the value and separates every three digits with commas.

After these subtotals are printed, the variables SUBSAL and SUBEMP must be set to zero so that the next department's totals can be calculated:

SUBSAL = 0;
SUBEMP = 0;

The next statement checks for the final observation and prints the grand totals:

IF FINAL THEN PUT // '*GRAND TOTALS' @31 'EMPLOYEES = ' TOTEMP**
  @55 'SALARY = ' TOTSAL DOLLAR10.2;

This finishes our program, which looks like this:

```
DATA WEEKLY;
   INPUT NAME $ EMPL__NO DEPT SALARY;
   CARDS;
data lines
PROC SORT;
   BY DEPT NAME;
DATA __NULL__;
   SET WEEKLY END = FINAL;
   BY DEPT;
   FILE PRINT;
   TITLE 'DEPARTMENT SALARIES';
   IF __N__ = 1 THEN PUT / @6 'DEPT' @18 'EMPLOYEE NUMBER'
      @43 'NAME' @61 'SALARY';
   IF __N__ = 1 THEN PUT
         '- - - - - - - - - - - - - - - - - - - - - - - - - - - - - - - - - - - - - - - - - - -';
   SUBSAL + SALARY;
   TOTSAL + SALARY;
   SUBEMP + 1;
   TOTEMP + 1;
   PUT DEPT 6-8 EMPL__NO 24-27 @ 43 NAME SALARY 59-66 .2;
   IF LAST.DEPT;
   PUT / '***DEPARTMENT  ' DEPT 'TOTALS' @31 'EMPLOYEES = '
      SUBEMP @55 'SALARY = ' SUBSAL DOLLAR10.2 / ;
   SUBSAL = 0;
   SUBEMP = 0;
   IF FINAL THEN PUT // '***GRAND TOTALS' @31 'EMPLOYEES = '
      TOTEMP @55 'SALARY = ' TOTSAL DOLLAR10.2;
```

The report produced appears in figure 13-9.

---

[1] "IF FINAL THEN..." and "IF FINAL = 1 THEN..." are equivalent because a value of 1 is considered *true*, a value of 0 *false*.

Getting Started:
The SAS® System
at Your Installation
by Alice Allen

Starting with questions
Finding the SAS System
Seeing results
Calling for help

The SAS System works with many different arrangements of computer hardware and software. Since this book applies generally to a wide range of systems, you will have to discover certain facts about your computing environment on your own. If you are already experienced with the computer on which you plan to execute SAS programs, you can skip this appendix. Otherwise, you can begin using the SAS System only after you know the answers to the questions in this appendix. If you need assistance, your local SAS Software Consultant is a good source of information. (Fill in the blanks for future reference.)

SAS Software Consultant _____ Phone _____
Other Systems Personnel _____ Phone _____
_____ Phone _____
_____ Phone _____

Starting with questions

What kind of input device will you use to communicate with your computer?
One type of input device is a computer terminal with a keyboard for entering text and commands. Some terminals print on paper rolls; others have screens where text is displayed.

```
┌─────────────────────────────────────────────────────────────────────┐
│                                                                       │
│   Terminal (model, notes) _____    │
│                                                                       │
│   _____    │
│                                                                       │
│   _____    │
│                                                                       │
│   _____    │
│                                                                       │
└─────────────────────────────────────────────────────────────────────┘
```

In some instances what you can do with SAS software depends on the capabilities of your input device. For this reason, you must master the basics of the input method you plan to use before you try to master SAS programming. For example, knowing the functions of your terminal's keys is essential from the beginning.

Another method is to enter a SAS program on keypunched cards; the input device is a card reader attached to the computer.

What is the name of the operating system that executes the SAS System on your computer? The *operating system* is the software that controls the activities of the computer, including access to the SAS System. You will use the operating system's control language to request SAS software.

```
┌─────────────────────────────────────────────────────────────────────┐
│                                                                       │
│   Machine _____    │
│   Operating System (name) _____    │
│                                                                       │
└─────────────────────────────────────────────────────────────────────┘
```

SAS literature classifies operating systems into the following categories: AOS/VS, CMS, OS, PRIMOS, VM/PC, VMS, and VSE. Learn the name of your operating system at this point. If the name of your operating system does not match any of these terms, find out into which category your operating system falls.

Which is the best execution mode available to you for your task? *Execution mode* describes the specific way you submit programs to be processed. The execution mode you choose depends on the capabilities of your input device, the alternatives available with your operating system, and what you want the SAS System to do.

Generally, if you have a large amount of data that is already entered, you will be able to consider *batch mode*; for example, a monthly payroll is often processed in batch. Programs on keypunched cards are executed in batch mode, and batch mode is available from terminals on some operating systems. If you must have information processed as soon as it is entered, you work from a terminal in *interactive mode*. Airline flight reservation systems and automatic teller transactions at banks require interactive mode, also called *conversational mode*.

```
┌─────────────────────────────────────────────────────────────────────┐
│                                                                       │
│   Execution  Mode _____    │
│                                                                       │
└─────────────────────────────────────────────────────────────────────┘
```

Given your operating system's batch or interactive modes, which SAS modes of execution are available to you? There are four execution modes available with the SAS System as shown in **Figure A1.1**, although all modes may not be available locally on your operating system. You can choose different execution modes for different SAS applications.

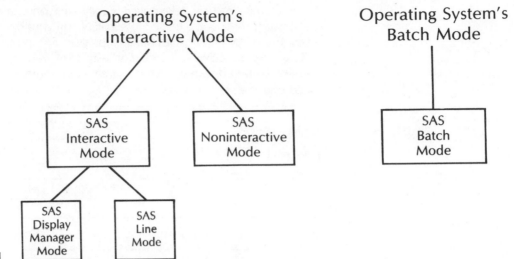

figure A1-1

A *batch SAS job* is submitted to the computer and waits its turn for execution along with the jobs of other users on the operating system. If you are using a terminal, you prepare a file containing statements in the operating system's control language and all the SAS program statements for the job, or you can prepare a similar deck of keypunched cards to be read. The example at the end of Chapter 1 was run as a batch SAS job.

A *noninteractive SAS session* also requires you to prepare a file containing SAS program statements without control statements; however, this job is submitted to the system for immediate rather than batch execution.

During an *interactive line-mode SAS session*, you enter SAS statements one or several at a time, and the system responds to each statement.

If you have a terminal on which the SAS System supports full-screen capability, you can take advantage of the features of an *interactive SAS display manager session*. SAS display manager is a set of screens and special commands for entering SAS programs and viewing results simultaneously. Among other advantages, the display manager method combines the best features of interactive line mode and noninteractive mode. The SAS Display Manager System is described in the *SAS User's Guide: Basics, Version 5 Edition*.

Before you access SAS software, you need to decide which execution methods are available and which one best suits your immediate needs. The SAS Software Consultant will be aware of any local requirements or restrictions.

SAS Execution Modes (check if available)

_____ SAS Batch Mode

_____ SAS Noninteractive Mode

_____ SAS Line Mode

_____ SAS Display Manager

Which text editor available on your operating system will you use to prepare files for SAS programs? With SAS batch mode from a terminal and SAS noninteractive mode you must learn how to type program statements into a file on your operating system using an *editor*. (The SAS display manager has a built-in editor.)

An editor is a set of commands, some possibly assigned to terminal keys, for entering and changing text. Ask your SAS Software Consultant or operating system personnel to recommend a text editor available on your operating system, and practice using the editor before attempting to prepare SAS program statements.

Learning to use SAS software most effectively requires that you master your terminal's keyboard with operating system commands and with a text editor, if you need one, before you start.

Editor _____

Access Instructions _____

_____

_____

_____

Finding the SAS System

How do you get connected or log on to the operating system from your terminal? The first operating system command that you will learn is the *logon command*, which brings your user identification code to the attention of the operating system. The logon procedure varies from one computer installation to another, so you must ask how to log on.

Logon Instructions _____

_____

_____

_____

How do you get access to the SAS System? Similarly, the command you enter to request SAS access is different for different operating systems, execution modes, and installations. You must find out exactly which command to use from your SAS Software Consultant.

SAS System Access

SAS Batch Mode _____

SAS Noninteractive Mode _____

SAS Line Mode _____

SAS Display Manager _____

Seeing results

How will you receive the results of your SAS programs? As you become an experienced SAS user, you will probably use several different methods for getting SAS output for different applications.

Depending on execution mode, you receive the results of SAS programs on the terminal screen, in printed form, or in a computer file by default. Your computer facility may also have other local access methods your consultant can tell you about. If you are using SAS display manager with a full-screen terminal, you will be able to view the results of each program statement and any procedure output on special screens as soon as it is produced.

When you are ready to print the results, ask where output is printed by default. In addition, find out the control statements required to print the output on other devices in other locations, for example, a line printer in your department or a laser printer with high-quality results in another building.

Output devices (list, notes) _____

_____

_____

Calling for help   You can view a brief description of individual SAS features by using the SAS HELP statement. For example,

HELP PRINT;

provides a brief description of the PRINT procedure. The statement

HELP;

provides a list of topics for which help is available. (The HELP statement is most useful in interactive SAS line-mode and display manager sessions.)

Appendix 2

More about the SAS® System

What Is the SAS System?

The SAS System is a software system for data analysis. The goal of SAS Institute is to provide data analysts one system to meet all their computing needs. When your computing needs are met, you are free to concentrate on results rather than on the mechanics of getting them. Instead of learning programming languages, several statistical packages, and utility programs, you only need to learn the SAS System.

To the all-purpose base SAS software, you can add tools for graphics, forecasting, data entry, and interfaces to other data bases to provide one total system. SAS software runs on IBM 370/30xx/43xx and compatible machines in batch and interactively under OS and TSO, CMS, VSE, and SSX; on Digital Equipment Corporation VAX™ 11/7xx series under VMS;™ Data General ECLIPSE® series under AOS/VS and MV series under AOS/VS; Prime Series 50 under PRIMOS;® and IBM PC AT/370 and XT/370 under VM/PC. Note: not all products are available for all operating systems.

Base SAS software provides tools for:

- information storage and retrieval
- data modification and programming
- report writing
- statistical analysis
- file handling.

Information storage and retrieval The SAS System reads data values in virtually any form from cards, disk, or tape and then organizes the values into a SAS data set. The data can be combined with other SAS data sets using the file-handling operations described below. The data can be analyzed statistically and can be used to produce reports. SAS data sets are automatically self-documenting since they contain both the data values and their descriptions. The special structure of a SAS data library minimizes maintenance.

Data modification and programming A complete set of SAS statements and functions is available for modifying data. Some program statements perform standard operations such as creating new variables, accumulating totals, and checking for errors; others are powerful programming tools such as DO/END and IF-THEN/ELSE statements. The data-handling features are so valuable that base SAS software is used by many as a data base management system.

Report writing   Just as base SAS software reads data in almost any form, it can write data in almost any form. In addition to the preformatted reports that SAS procedures produce, SAS software users can design and produce printed reports in any form, as well as punched cards and output files.

Statistical analysis   The statistical analysis procedures in the SAS System are among the finest available. They range from simple descriptive statistics to complex multivariate techniques. Their designs are based on our belief that you should never need to tell the SAS System anything it can figure out by itself. Statistical integrity is thus accompanied by ease of use. Especially noteworthy statistical features are the linear model procedures, of which GLM (**G**eneral **L**inear **M**odels) is the flagship.

File handling   Combining values and observations from several data sets is often necessary for data analysis. SAS software has tools for editing, subsetting, concatenating, merging, and updating data sets. Multiple input files can be processed simultaneously, and several reports can be produced in one pass of the data.

Other SAS System Products

With base SAS software, you can integrate SAS software products for graphics, data entry, operations research, and interfaces to other data bases to provide one total system:

- SAS/FSP software—interactive, menu-driven facilities for data entry, editing, retrieval of SAS files, letter writing, and spreadsheet analysis
- SAS/GRAPH software—device-intelligent color graphics for business and research applications
- SAS/REPLAY-CICS software—interface that allows users of CICS/OS/VS and CICS/DOS/VS to store, manage, and replay SAS/GRAPH displays
- SAS/OR software—decision support tools for operations research and project management
- SAS/AF software—a full-screen, interactive applications facility
- SAS/ETS software—expanded tools for business analysis, forecasting, and financial planning
- SAS/IMS-DL/I software—interface for reading, updating, and writing IMS/VS or CICS DL/I data bases
- SAS/IML software—multi-level, interactive programming language whose data elements are matrices.

SAS Institute Documentation

Using this manual   Because the SAS System was designed as an all-purpose tool, many SAS features are needed only for special types of problems. You don't need to know everything in all our manuals to use SAS software. Most jobs use only a small subset of the information in the SAS System.

The *SAS Introductory Guide* contains the basic elements of SAS programming and gets you started quickly using the SAS System. As you become more experienced, you can use the other manuals and technical reports available from SAS Institute.

Other SAS Institute manuals and technical reports   The *SAS User's Guide: Basics* contains the fundamentals of the SAS System: an introduction to DATA and PROC steps; the syntax and use of SAS statements; macros; system options; and procedures for descriptive statistics, report writing, and utilities. *SAS User's Guide:*

Basics is the first of two volumes that are the primary documentation for base SAS software. The other volume is *SAS User's Guide: Statistics*, which contains the ANOVA and GLM procedures discussed in the *SAS Introductory Guide* as well as other advanced statistical procedures in the areas of regression, analysis of variance, discriminant analysis, clustering, and scoring.

Each of the other SAS System products has a user's guide. However, all products in the SAS System are based on the fundamental structures outlined in the *SAS Introductory Guide* and the *SAS Users' Guide: Basics*.

Since the SAS System operates under the control of the computer's operating system, you can do more with SAS software if you understand the interactions between the SAS System and the operating system. The SAS Companion series describes the interactions between SAS software and each operating system under which the SAS System runs.

SAS Institute also publishes other manuals you may find useful. The *SAS Applications Guide* deals with common data-handling applications, and several manuals on statistical applications are available.

The SAS Technical Report Series documents work in progress, describes new supplemental procedures, and covers a variety of applications areas. Some of the` features described in these reports are still in experimental form and are not yet available as SAS procedures.

Write to SAS Institute for a current publications catalog, which describes the manuals as well as technical reports and lists their prices.

If you have any problems with this manual, please take time to write to SAS Institute. We will consider your suggestions for future editions. In the meantime, ask your installation's SAS Software Consultant for help.

SAS release?   To find out which release of SAS software you are using, run any SAS job and look at the release number in the notes at the beginning of the SAS log.

SAS Services to Users

Technical support   SAS Institute supports users through the Technical Support Department. If you have a problem running a SAS job, you should contact your site's SAS Software Consultant. If the problem cannot be resolved locally, your local support personnel should call the Institute's Technical Support Department at (919) 467-8000 on weekdays between 9:00 a.m. and 5:00 p.m. Eastern Standard Time. A brochure describing the services provided by the Technical Support Department is available from SAS Institute.

Training   SAS Institute sponsors a comprehensive training program, including programs of study for novice data processors, statisticians, applications programmers, systems programmers, and local support personnel. *SAS Training*, a semi-annual training publication, describes the total training program and each course currently being offered by SAS Institute.

News magazine   *SAS Communications* is the quarterly news magazine of SAS Institute. Each issue contains ideas for more effective use of the SAS System, information about research and development underway at SAS Institute, the current training schedule, new publications, and news of the SAS Users Group International (SUGI).

To receive *SAS Communications* regularly, send your name and complete address to:

SAS Institute Mailing List
SAS Institute Inc.
Box 8000
Cary, NC 27511-8000

Sample library   Each SAS site receives a data set containing sample SAS programs on the base SAS software installation tape. The programs illustrate features of SAS procedures and creative SAS programming techniques that can help you gain an in-depth knowledge of SAS capabilities.

Here are a few examples of programs included:

ANOVA	analyzing a Latin-square split-plot design
CORR	getting correlations and saving the correlations in a SAS data set using PROC CORR
DATASHOW	creating and manipulating SAS data sets
MEANS	selecting additional statistics with PROC MEANS and saving the statistics in a SAS data set
PRINT	creating more detailed reports with PROC PRINT

Check with your SAS Software Consultant to find out how to access the sample programs.

SUGI   The SAS Users Group International (SUGI) is a nonprofit association of professionals who are interested in how others are using the SAS System. Although SAS Institute provides administrative support, SUGI is independent from the Institute. Membership is open to all users at SAS sites, and there is no membership fee.

Annual conferences are structured to allow many avenues of discussion. Users present invited and contributed papers on various topics, for example:

- computer performance evaluation and systems software
- econometrics and time series
- graphics
- information systems
- interactive techniques
- statistics
- tutorials in SAS System software.

Proceedings of the annual conferences are distributed to SUGI registrants. Extra copies may be purchased from SAS Institute.

SASware Ballot   SAS users provide valuable input toward the direction of future SAS development by ranking their priorities on the annual SASware Ballot. The top vote-getters are announced at the SUGI conference. Complete results of the SASware Ballot are also printed in the *SUGI Proceedings*.

Supplemental library   SAS users at many installations have written their own SAS procedures for a wide variety of specialized applications. Some of these user-written procedures are available through the SUGI supplemental library and are documented in the *SUGI Supplemental Library User's Guide*, although only a few procedures are supported by SAS Institute staff. (Note: not all operating systems support the SUGI supplemental library.)

Licensing the SAS System   The SAS System is licensed to customers in the Western Hemisphere from the Institute's headquarters in Cary, NC. To serve the needs of our international customers, the Institute maintains subsidiaries in the United Kingdom, New

Zealand, Australia, Singapore, Germany, and France. In addition, agents in other countries are licensed distributors for the SAS System. For a complete list of offices, write or call:

SAS Institute Inc.
SAS Circle
Box 8000
Cary, NC 27511-8000
(919) 476-8000

Index